KEN FOLLETT

Ken Follett. Photograph used with permission.

KEN FOLLETT

A Critical Companion

Richard C. Turner

CRITICAL COMPANIONS TO POPULAR CONTEMPORARY WRITERS
Kathleen Gregory Klein, Series Editor

Greenwood Press
Westport, Connecticut • London

Library of Congress Cataloging-in-Publication Data

Turner, Richard Charles.
    Ken Follett : a critical companion / Richard C. Turner.
      p. cm.—(Critical companions to popular contemporary
writers, ISSN 1082–4979)
    Includes bibliographical references (p.) and index.
    ISBN 0–313–29415–1 (alk. paper)
    1. Follett, Ken—Criticism and interpretation. I. Title.
II. Series.
    PR6056.045Z78   1996
    823'.914—dc20   96–18206

British Library Cataloguing in Publication Data is available.

Library of Congress Catalog Card Number: 96–18206
ISBN: 0–313–29415–1
ISSN: 1082–4979

First published in 1996

Greenwood Press, 88 Post Road West, Westport, CT 06881
An imprint of Greenwood Publishing Group, Inc.

Printed in the United States of America

∞

The paper used in this book complies with the
Permanent Paper Standard issued by the National
Information Standards Organization (Z39.48–1984).

10 9 8 7 6 5 4 3 2 1

For William, the Child of My Right Hand

Contents

Contents

Series Foreword

The authors who appear in the series Critical Companions to Popular Contemporary Writers are all best-selling writers. They do not have only one successful novel but a string of them. Fans, critics, and specialist readers eagerly anticipate their next book. For some, high cash advances and breakthrough sales figures are automatic; movie deals often follow. Some writers become household names, recognized by almost everyone.

But novels are read one by one. Each reader chooses to start and, more important, to finish a book because of what she or he finds there. The real test of a novel is in the satisfaction its readers experience. This series acknowledges the extraordinary involvement of readers and writers in creating a best-seller.

The authors included in this series were chosen by an Advisory Board composed of high school English teachers and high school and public librarians. They ranked a list of best-selling writers according to their popularity among different groups of readers. Writers in the top-ranked group who had not received book-length, academic literary analysis (or none in at least the past ten years) were chosen for the series. Because of this selection method, Critical Companions to Popular Contemporary Writers meets a need that is not addressed elsewhere.

The volumes in the series are written by scholars with particular expertise in analyzing popular fiction. These specialists add an academic focus to the popular success that the best-selling writers already enjoy.

The series is designed to appeal to a wide range of readers. The general reading public will find explanations for the appeal of these well-known writers. Fans will find biographical and fictional questions answered. Students will find literary analysis, discussions of fictional genres, carefully organized introductions to new ways of reading the novels, and bibliographies for additional research. Students will also be able to apply what they have learned from this book to their readings of future novels by these best-selling writers.

Each volume begins with a biographical chapter drawing on published information, autobiographies or memoirs, prior interviews, and, in some cases, interviews given especially for this series. A chapter on literary history and genres describes how the author's work fits into a larger literary context. The following chapters analyze the writer's most important, most popular, and most recent novels in detail. Each chapter focuses on a single novel. This approach, suggested by the Advisory Board as the most useful to student research, allows for an in-depth analysis of the writer's fiction. Close and careful readings with numerous examples show readers exactly how the novels work. These chapters are organized around three central elements: plot development (how the story line moves forward), character development (what the reader knows about the important figures), and theme (the significant ideas of the novel). Chapters may also include sections on generic conventions (how the novel is similar to or different from others in its same category of science fiction, fantasy, thriller, etc.), narrative point of view (who tells the story and how), symbols and literary language, and historical or social context. Each chapter ends with an "alternative reading" of the novel. The volume concludes with a primary and secondary bibliography, including reviews.

The Alternative Readings are a unique feature of this series. By demonstrating a particular way of reading each novel, they provide a clear example of how a specific perspective can reveal important aspects of the book. In each alternative reading section, one contemporary literary theory—such as feminist criticism, Marxism, new historicism, deconstruction, or Jungian psychological critique—is defined in brief, easily comprehensible language. That definition is then applied to the novel to highlight specific features that might go unnoticed or be understood differently in a more general reading of the novel. Each volume defines two or three specific theories, making them part of the reader's understanding of how diverse meanings may be constructed from a single novel.

Taken collectively, the volumes in the Critical Companions to Popular

Contemporary Writers series provide a wide-ranging investigation of the complexities of current best-selling fiction. By treating these novels seriously as both literary works and publishing successes, the series demonstrates the potential of popular literature in contemporary culture.

Kathleen Gregory Klein
Southern Connecticut State University

Acknowledgments

Writing an extended critical treatment of a popular novelist such as Ken Follett offers a literary scholar an opportunity to test many of the claims made for literary criticism against the habits and received attitudes of the academy. On the one hand, literary criticism asks to be taken seriously because its work advances the understanding of cultural products such as novels and enables its readers to become better readers of novels and more powerful participants in the conversations about what is important in life. This work can support its claims easily when literary criticism treats the traditional canon. On the other hand, as the growing call for taking seriously works outside the traditional canon challenges literary criticism to find new bases for its claims, literary criticism needs to expand its vision of its work. Popular writing offers an occasion for literary criticism to bring its expertise to bear upon the work that currently compels the attention of readers who are themselves the participants in contemporary culture. If literary criticism is to make good its claims for its usefulness, then readings of popular writings offer a valuable site for those considerations. Thus, writing about Ken Follett represents a chance to bring the academy's concerns to a larger public.

It is to the academy, then, that I am grateful for the opportunity to do the work contained in this book. What contributions I make to the understanding of Ken Follett's work owe their origins to the teachers, students, and colleagues who have, over the years, expected that I would bring to bear the best of my intellectual resources on the issues and concerns under discussion in classes, in colloquia, and in scholarly presentations and articles. More immediately, I am grateful to my colleagues for the time and space they have given me during the past two years to get this book done. I am grateful as well for the patience and help I have received from Barbara Rader of Greenwood Press. The invitation from Kathleen Gregory Klein, the Series Editor, to do this book is only the latest in a long series of gifts and gestures of support I have received from her as a colleague and friend. It turns out that none of my long training and practice in the study of language and literature has prepared me to thank adequately Sandra Turner, whose support and love in this and in all my projects exceeds any ordinary measure and becomes itself a measure of the special grace she has brought to our lives.

KEN FOLLETT

The Life and Career of
Ken Follett

Ken Follett had the purest of motives when he began writing fiction: he did it for money. Before *Eye of the Needle* (1978) became a smash hit and made him a successful writer, he had been working as a crime reporter for a sensationalist London tabloid, the *Evening News*, assigned to dull court reporting rather than the respectable crime journalism he had hoped to do. But his car broke down one day, requiring money for repairs, and his second child had just been born, so he started writing novels. The famous eighteenth-century writer Samuel Johnson said once that no one but a blockhead writes for any reason other than money, and so Follett would appear to have that literary giant's blessing on his motives for entering a literary career. Follett's first novel, *The Big Needle* (1974), brought him an advance large enough to pay his car repair bills and confidence enough to quit his job as a reporter and take a new one at a publishing firm, Everest House. One of his reasons for seeking the publishing job was to find out how books become best-sellers and what he had to do to write one. So, Follett's career began with not only the impulse to write books that would sell but also to write books that would be best-sellers. His ambition turned very quickly to wanting to be an outstanding writer. Follett does not at all mind being labeled a "popular" writer because he derives great satisfaction from being one of the best at such writing.

THE DEVELOPMENT OF A WRITER

Although Follett's decision to write novels such as *Eye of the Needle* had been precipitous, his interest in thrillers goes back to his childhood. He began his interest in thrillers early, reading H. G. Wells by the age of seven and becoming a fan of Ian Fleming's James Bond novels by the time he was eleven. Follett has described himself as a child who spent a lot of time in fantasy worlds. Born 5 July 1949, he grew up in a middle-class household in Cardiff, Wales, and then in London. That household included his father, Martin, a clerk in the British internal revenue collection department, his mother, Lavinia, who kept the house, and his sister, Hannah. He attended publicly supported schools and entered the University of London at eighteen. Very soon after entering the university, he married Mary Elston, and they had their first son, Emanuele, soon thereafter. Mrs. Follett worked as a bookkeeper while Follett finished his degree and cared for their son. He graduated with an honors degree in philosophy in 1970 and took a job as a reporter and rock music columnist for the *South Wales Echo*, a Cardiff newspaper, where he worked until 1973. That year he took the job at the *Evening News* in London. The Folletts divorced in 1985.

Once Follett started writing novels, he did so with a passion, writing nine books and a children's book before the publication of *Eye of the Needle*. His first two spy novels—*The Shakeout* (1975) and *The Bear Raid* (1976)—focus on industrial espionage, a subject that was drawing a lot of important attention in Europe and America at the time but not enough to gain a following for the novels. During this period Follett wrote a number of novels under pseudonyms, including *The Big Needle*, *The Big Black* (1974), and *The Big Hit* (1975) under the name Symon Myles; *The Modigliani Scandal* (1976) and *Paper Money* (1977) under the name Zachary Stone; *The Power Twins and the Worm Puzzle* (1976) under the name Martin Martinsen; and *Amok: King of Legend* (1976) and *Capricorn One* (1978) under the name Bernard L. Ross. (*The Big Needle*, *The Modigliani Scandal*, and *Paper Money* have been reissued recently under Ken Follett's name.) Most of these early novels were murder mysteries or crime novels and drew upon the stories he had covered as a reporter. He wrote these novels at night while he worked at Everest House during the day, becoming deputy managing director in 1976. Follett told an interviewer that writing in this period had become a hobby for him and he likened his writing to the vegetables that other men grow in their spare time,

although he allowed that his novels sold for a good bit more than vegetables do (*Contemporary Authors* 150).

Follett had enough confidence in *Eye of the Needle* to resign from his
publishing job before the manuscript was accepted. His agent sold it to
Arbor House the day after Follett's resignation, and that sale changed
Follett's fortunes. Arbor House aggressively marketed the novel and sold
the paperback rights to an American publisher for a lucrative $800,000.
Including other related contracts, Follett earned $525,000 and overnight
became a premier novelist. The novel won the prestigious Edgar Award
from the Mystery Writers of America and was very favorably reviewed
by both American and British critics. He published another novel, *Triple*
(1979), with Arbor House and then signed a $3 million deal with New
American Library for his next three books.

Follett's relationships with his publishers share some of the excitement
and suspense of his novels. After he left Arbor House, he got into a legal
battle with them because they wanted to publish under his name a book
that he had rewritten or edited (the issue in the controversy). The United
States district judge who presided over the lawsuit Follett filed decided
in favor of Arbor House, ruling that the work Follett did amounted to
substantial rewriting and allowed the book to be published under the
names Ken Follett and René Louise Maurice, the pseudonym of the three
French journalists who had written the original version of the book.

Follett's publishing history made the news again in 1990 when he
signed a contract with Dell Publishing Company to write two books for
them for $12.3 million. The book deal generated extensive controversy
among publishers and writers because the enormous advances paid to
Follett and to Jeffrey Archer, another popular British writer, seemed to
inaugurate a Hollywood-like star system among best-selling writers.
John LeCarré worried that the big money would cause writers to lose
sight of their professional responsibilities to readers and to publishers.
Robert Ludlum's editor huffed that, if Follett and Archer got such large
advances, then Ludlum and other writers who outsell them ought to get
even bigger advances (*New York Times*, 16 July 1990). The uproar over
these advances called attention to publishers moving into the world of
big business and the need for them to compete for sales in the bookstores
of large chains and other mass-market venues. The famous names of
best-sellers such as Ken Follett improve their chances of entry into these
markets and so justify the huge advances, although the practice risks
turning books into commodities. Follett claimed that the high price was
well justified, a sentiment echoed by Dell publishing. This astronomical

figure suggests how prominent Ken Follett has become in the world of book publishing and how substantial his work has become. He went into the business to make money and he has done that with a vengeance. The response to his work by readers and reviewers suggests that there is more to his success than just financial gain, but the financial gain is indeed significant.

Follett's sweetheart deal with Dell resulted in the very successful *A Dangerous Fortune* (1993), but it went a little sour as he began his second novel under the contract, *A Place Called Freedom* (1995). Dell is said to have objected to a book with a setting in the era of the American Revolution and Follett resented the intrusion on his authorial prerogatives. Follett and his agent, Al Zuckerman, eventually worked out a contract with Crown Publishers to pick up the rest of the Dell obligation for the historical novel and a new agreement for two more books. Follett, for all his delight in profit and lucrative book contracts, insists that his books come out under terms that represent his own best sense of what they should be, and he is said to have lost as much as $1 million by breaking the contract with Dell.

In 1985 Follett married the former Barbara Broer and now lives in a two hundred-year-old house overlooking the Thames River in the Chelsea district of London with the two children from his first marriage and the three children from her first marriage. He keeps a second residence in New York. He likes fine wines, excellent cooking, and expensive and fashionable clothes. He likes to read other novelists—classics of the Great Tradition such as Jane Austen, George Eliot, Charles Dickens, and Anthony Trollope; the present-day American novelists Pat Conroy and Larry McMurtry; and the Latin American novelists Gabriel Garcia Marquez, Jorge Amado, and Isabel Allende. He loves Shakespeare and is an avid fan of the Royal Shakespeare Company. His other pursuits include playing bass guitar in a band called Damn Right I Got the Blues. A liberal in politics, he has authored a pamphlet on injustice in the British immigration laws.

KEN FOLLETT ON LITERATURE AND LIFE

Ken Follett describes his novels as different from ordinary thrillers in that he places less emphasis on hardware such as weapons, airplanes, and fast cars and concentrates more on character development, especially women characters, who are rare in thrillers. He takes great pride in the fact that his thrillers feature strong women in important roles with the result that his work reaches many more women than ordinary thrillers do. Follett is fond of pointing out that people tell him that the character of Jane Lambert in *Lie Down with Lions* (1986) is very much like his second wife or at least very much like the person Follett first thought Barbara was. He points to Augusta Pilaster in *A Dangerous Fortune* as one of the best female characters he has created, even though she is far from the novel's heroine and is perhaps the most malevolent presence in the book. Because of this success in pushing the boundaries of the usual format of this type of book, Follett feels free to try out new genres, as he did in *The Pillars of Wisdom* (1989) and *A Dangerous Fortune*, or in stretching his already successful genre, as he did in *Night over Water* (1991) or in the earlier experiments with thrillers. Follett is committed to being popular and accessible to his readers, but he enjoys the challenge of leaving mainstream expectations and inducing his many readers to follow him.

Follett describes writing as a challenging and difficult calling, one that he pursues with energy and dedication. He spends a considerable amount of time writing out a detailed outline and then a much shorter time writing the story from the outline. For instance, the outline for *The Pillars of Wisdom* took him eighteen months to write. He revises his first drafts, but usually not more than once, although he might rewrite an individual section many times to get it right. He works from nine in the morning to four in the afternoon each day that he is home, producing about a thousand words of publishable text. Writing requires him to devote constant attention to a work for months without any time off except for an occasional weekend. He complains about the demands that book promotions make on his time and the rigors that traveling requires. For novels set in historical periods, he does extensive and meticulous research and, at times, enlists the aid of research assistants to cover the range of research information he needs. He asks family members to give him feedback on his ideas and early versions of his text. He says that his son told him that in an early version of *A Dangerous Fortune*, Maisie was too much a victim to be convincing as a heroine, and so he changed the plot to avoid that fault. He describes his research methods as a combination of general "fishing expeditions," an approach that takes a broad look at the gathered information with a confidence that details that catch his eye will be useful at some point in the writing, and the specific searches for the exact detail that will carry the authenticity of the story and for which researchers are especially helpful. Follett has paid a lot of attention to his craft and he is determined to ensure that his books have an impact. He has certainly influenced millions of readers. He has developed his own approach to his art, which suggests a talent ready to master challenges and explore experimental directions.

Follett's interest in historical settings for his novels arises from an assumption that people in other historical periods are more or less like people today, and that assumption makes historical periods rich sources of reflection for present-day readers. In the historical thrillers from *Eye of the Needle* to *Lie Down with Lions* Follett presents actual historical situations in which an individual, not too unlike the reader at first glance, could have made a difference in the course of history. That possibility intrigues both Follett and his reader because of the overwhelming likelihood that events and previously determined movements shape the course of the lives of individuals, nations, and cultures. Follett has addressed the connection between individual choice and circumstances beyond any one's control in a number of his books; he talks about his view on this connection in the Introduction to the reissued *The Modigliani Scandal*:

> In a modern thriller the hero generally saves the world. Traditional adventure stories are more modest: The central character merely saves his own life, and perhaps the life of a faithful friend or a plucky girl. In less sensational novels—the middlebrow, well-told narratives that have been the staple diet of readers for more than a century—there is less at stake, but still a character's efforts, struggles and choices determine his destiny in a dramatic fashion. I don't actually believe that life is like that. In reality, circumstances quite beyond our control usually determine whether we live or die, become happy or miserable, strike it rich or lose everything. (7)

Follett only rarely discusses the philosophical dimensions of his writing in this manner, although his novels regularly address philosophical perspectives.

Follett often sidesteps questions that invite him to enter into critical discussions of the meaning of his works. He is serious about his work, but he professes to be puzzled about what critics might find to say about it. He maintains that he is not the best judge of the significance of his books. He points out that his approach to writing does not encourage spending much time thinking about meaning: he finds an intriguing subject and then just follows the directions that the story and the characters seem to want to pursue. He sees this habit of writing as consistent with his personality and his approach to life: things happen to people, in stories and in life, which compel his attention and become material for his books. He acknowledges that this approach often presents difficulties for the marketing people at publishing houses because they cannot predict the thrust of his upcoming books and so cannot easily package him for presentation to the buying public. He acknowledges that his stories explore moral concerns and values and he does not shy away from their serious implications, but he simply does not find it useful to explain himself.

Follett takes a skeptical attitude toward the critical attention he is receiving and toward his celebrity as one of the world's best-selling authors. He does not seem to change his approach to writing books in response to either critical attention or fame. He does change directions in his writing when he has exhausted his imagination in a given type of book. If he feels he has gone stale, then he looks around in a new area for a story that will grab his attention. After he finished *Lie Down with Lions*, he had the feeling that he had nothing new to say in the thriller format, so he returned to an earlier idea for writing a book about cathedrals and developed it into *The Pillars of the Earth*. His most recent project focuses on a young woman who is working as a geneticist on studies of twins. He became interested in this project as he began thinking about the power and presence of technology, especially genetic engineering, in present-day society. This project has some suspense and a chase in it, but it is not a thriller in the manner of his previous books.

Follett does pay attention to the field within which he works and watches the reception given to other popular writers to ensure that his stories continue to be gripping and exciting. He has noted, for instance, that some recent popular novelists use fewer explicit lovemaking scenes than he usually does, or than might have been expected in popular fiction twenty years ago. Because he sees the explicit sex in his novels as central and important to their success, he expects to continue writing about sex in the same way (Interview, 22 May 1995). Follett watches his field carefully and reads widely; his determination to write stories as he chooses does not exclude adjusting his sense of what a reader will find exciting and interesting.

Early Writings
and *On Wings of Eagles*
(1983)

Ken Follett's career as a best-selling novelist starts with *Eye of the Needle*, but his writing career began five years earlier. The early books provided practice for Follett, but some of them stand also as novelistic achievements on their own. The early novels reveal elements that Follett used well from the start and some that he left behind as he found his special strengths and his artistic stride.

THE BIG NEEDLE (1974)

The Big Needle, the novel that Ken Follett wrote in such a hurry to earn the money to repair his car, offers insight into the shape his career has taken. The novel presents a clear and lively adventure that engages the reader's interest in both the outcome of the plot and the ability of the good guy to make it back in one piece. By placing the action in the hands of an independent operator who makes his own rules as he goes, it avoids the need for the writer to be convincing in terms of accurate and precise details about how a large spy or government organization works. A reader who makes a commitment to this character is swept up in the suspense of the chase both when the good guy chases his objective and when he himself is chased.

The Big Needle focuses on the worst nightmare of many parents since widely available drugs have emerged as a threat to the health of young people and the safety of society. The main character, Chad "Apples" Carstairs, is called into action when he hears that his teenage daughter is in a coma caused by a drug overdose. Unable to do anything for his daughter, he turns his rage on the drug trade and plots to wreak havoc on it as a form of revenge as well as a civic duty. His private mission takes him through some of the seamier sides of London low life, to the drug capitals of southern France, and back to London. He involves his close personal companions in these activities and encounters some minor characters along the way. Carstairs encounters some brutal opposition and personal betrayal in his pursuit of his plan. His plot brings about a change in his sense of values and leads him to an affirmation of a new lifestyle that eschews his former, pleasure-oriented life for another chance at fulfilling the traditional role of father, which he had side-stepped earlier. He succeeds with his revenge and effects a change in his life, two outcomes that the reader can applaud. Carstairs's actions overcome the 1970s nightmare and enable him to begin a productive and admirable life unaffected by the social and cultural forces shaping the age.

Point of View

Chad Carstairs, the first-person narrator, tells his own story in *The Big Needle* with confidence, assurance, and a sense of his own importance and cleverness. He announces his circumstances with clear-eyed and direct honesty, even though those circumstances include a number of aspects that are likely to shock and puzzle the casual reader. As Carstairs refers to waking up in bed with a beautiful Jamaican bisexual woman and another bisexual woman, who is a titled aristocrat, the reader might appreciate his openness about his personal commitments, but only a few readers will find the narrator's position familiar. This novel starts off with an extraordinary grouping and creates the expectation in the reader that an even more extraordinary narrative is to follow.

Character Development

The most prominent character in *The Big Needle* is the narrator, Carstairs. His direct and forceful personality is important for the credibility of the narration and the pace at which the novel will move to pursue its adventure and solve its mystery. Carstairs is a successful businessman who has, he tells the reader, an interesting background: "Most people think my Cockney accent is for real and my BBC English faked. In fact it's the other way around. I was born into a classy family which went bankrupt. When I switched from public school to an East End secondary school the first thing I learned was to talk like the other kids. Another useful tactic was to fight first and ask what it was all about afterwards" (34). This introduction of himself as being made up of surprising contrasts makes him perfect as the hero of a crime adventure. He can draw on unusual resources and still maintain credibility because he has this rich and varied background. He establishes himself as a person who always seeks to win and is willing to do whatever it takes to win. His revelation about his tough background and his hard-boiled rise to success enables the story to get off to a quick start so that the reader can accept the daring and impulsive decision he makes to go after the head of the heroin ring supplying London. The reader knows Carstairs has the resources to make such a decision from the telephone conversation he has with his secretary in which he announces he will be gone for a few days and leaves four separate multimillion-dollar deals confidently in her hands. This independence in the face of such high stakes tells the reader that Carstairs will certainly push the adventure where it needs to go. He has a sensitive side as well. He makes it clear that he is devoted to his two house companions, although he also states that their satisfactory relationship is built on a series of insecurities and dependencies. He cares for his daughter and honestly regrets his failures to keep in touch with her. He quickly reads people except when he acts out of anger or hate; then he is not very perceptive and usually pays the consequences. Indeed, Carstairs's series of mistakes emphasizes his lack of experience in hunting criminals and his amateur status as the hero of this adventure, a consideration very important to the reader's investment of sympathy and interest in this character.

Most of the other characters are minor, determined by the brevity of the story and the simplicity of the plot. The two most prominent are Carstairs's lovers and house companions, Babs and Annabel. They accompany him on parts of his mission and at times share in the danger. Babs is kidnaped and tortured once and raped at another time. These two women appear to the reader in much the same way that Carstairs describes them, and so the reader need not look very hard at their function in the story. Carstairs even anticipates their decisions to leave him at the end of the novel.

Carstairs spends a significant portion of time with another minor character, Guy House, an American adventurer who joins him in the plot to deceive the heroin dealers in France. House represents well a skeptical attitude toward mainstream values prevalent in the 1970s, which echoes Carstairs's own attitudes. House's belief that experience and action are the only things that a person can count on takes Carstairs's own thrill-seeking attitude a step further. House's clear and casual disdain for danger makes his eventual death at the hands of the drug dealers problematic for the reader. If House's life meant so little, first to him and then to the drug dealers, the reader may experience some doubt about the strong and unqualified regard for life evident in other characters and used by the novelist to capture the reader's sympathy. The conflict arises from the extreme shift in the attitude toward life in one character compared to another.

House has another interesting function in the novel: he gives a rationale for the reader's interest in the development of the story. When Carstairs asks House why he has agreed to help him, House responds, "The rest of it [the reason] is mystery, and you're the mystery. You're no professional dope dealer—you haven't the marks of it, you don't know enough about it, and you're the wrong temperament. You're a straight businessman—well, fairly straight. You've got a secret motive for this whole thing, and I want to follow through until I find out what it is" (54). House spells out many of the reasons readers continue to stay with this and other novels and so affirms the reader's persistence and encourages continuation. Follett offers this indirect model for his own readers on how to read his books.

Other minor characters include corrupt police, loyal crime reporters, denizens of the shadow world between the rich and powerful and the criminal elements of society, and the range of criminals themselves. Carstairs's former wife and his daughter appear briefly. His daughter figures prominently at the beginning as the reason he goes after the drug dealers and at the end when she becomes the occasion for Carstairs to give up his sybaritic life and settle on a farm.

Plot Development

The Big Needle begins as a revenge story. Carstairs reacts immediately and viscerally to news that his daughter is in a coma owing to a drug overdose and immediately resolves to punish the heroin dealers who supplied her with drugs. He maintains this dedication throughout the novel, although that resolve pauses for sexual encounters at regular intervals during the narrative. He wonders at times about the wisdom of an amateur like himself taking on such a difficult and dangerous task, but his hesitations are short-lived and he never backs down.

Some of the plot turns address the author's concern with values. The presence of sexual adventures adds to the sense of value conflicts that engage readers. At an amazingly fast rate, Carstairs's pursuit of his plan takes him to scenes of exotic sexual activity. The episodes are not exactly gratuitous, but they seem to linger longer than the barebones plot requires. The novel begins with an announcement of the hero's sexual liberation that seems to be an epitome of the sexual revolution of the 1970s. But that hedonistic and self-indulgent approach to pleasure and excitement is at odds with the paternal love and protectiveness that consume Carstairs when he hears about his daughter's overdose. The novel's continued engagement with solipsistic personal relationships becomes a greater and greater contrast to the commitment to duty evident in other characters. Finally, Carstairs's plans to retire for two or three years to a rural farm with his daughter and his matchmaking efforts amount to a complete turnaround for him. The reader, convinced by the novel that Carstairs is a proven winner and a person of determination, is sure that the hero can and should make this change. The ending then stands in sharp but convincing contrast to the novel's opening. The business of the plot is to complete the plan Carstairs formulates to get revenge and to set up a change in his character and the world of the novel that suggests to the reader that this revenge led in at least some respects to a better world.

Thematic Issues

The most prominent feature of *The Big Needle* is its presentation of a world almost entirely lacking in meaningful public structures or values. The only order in this world comes from within and the only values arise from personal decisions and idiosyncratic codes. Carstairs never once thinks of going to the authorities to ask for justice for his daughter. He believes in justice, but he assumes that he is the only one to pursue it. He does not rail against the incompetence or corruption of public institutions; he just finds them irrelevant to the culture of money and power that seems to dominate the world he lives in and within which he has proven himself to be successful. His decision to seek revenge himself is an extension of his exertion of power and determination in the business world.

All the characters in *The Big Needle* operate in a world without governmental authority or admirable public goals. Meaning arises from personal integrity and personal interest alone. At an important moment Carstairs decides to pursue his mission because, in addition to revenging his daughter, his actions will save at least a few hundred young Londoners from getting hooked on heroin. But this thought is as close as anyone comes in this novel to a sense of public value or public virtue. Even a casual glance at Carstairs's thinking reveals the flaws in his suggestion and the inadequacy of even a determined individual like himself to provide a protected environment for others. But the novel leaves that kind of reasoning off to the side so that the adventure can be told. The story works, but the implications of the actions cannot exclude the creeping feeling that the world of *The Big Needle* is grim and dangerous. As an adventure the novel succeeds, but it also reveals the author's concern for the lack of structure and value in the modern world.

THE MODIGLIANI SCANDAL (1976)

The Modigliani Scandal is a complex book because it is both a fast-paced crime caper and a serious look at the place of art in modern life. The crime caper part has the comedic structure of young and rebellious artists tricking an older and rigid art establishment in order to teach it a lesson. Another plot line follows a knowledgeable young scholar dogged by older, corrupt collectors in a search for a lost art masterpiece. The twists and complications in the plot keep the reader engaged in the game while the discussions about value in art and business keep the focus on concerns that are important in any age but were a special concern in the 1970s as the societies of industrialized nations responded to challenges from their youth to mainstream values and to the increasing difficulty in distinguishing between the authentic and the ersatz on canvas and in society.

In the Introduction to the reissue of *The Modigliani Scandal*, Ken Follett discusses his intentions in writing the novel and his evaluation of it from the vantage point of fifteen years' experience of writing novels. His comments focus on the balance between individual freedom and external forces that shape people's lives:

> In *The Modigliani Scandal* I tried to write a new kind of novel, one that would reflect the subtle subordination of individual freedom to more powerful machinery. In this immodest project I failed. It may be that such a novel cannot be written: Even if Life is not about individual choice, perhaps Literature is. . . . What I wrote, in the end, was a lighthearted crime story in which an assortment of people, mostly young, get up to a variety of capers, none of which turns out quite as expected. The critics praised it as sprightly, ebullient, light, bright, cheery, light (again), and fizzy. I was disappointed that they had not noted my serious intentions. (8)

Follett's summary of what critics said captures much of the quality of the novel as it is read. It is the work of interpretation to locate the serious intentions that Follett announces are part of the novel.

Point of View

The Modigliani Scandal is told by an omniscient narrator who knows everything that is going on in the plot as well as in the characters' minds. The story is told through dialogue and reflections on what the main characters are thinking. The lighthearted quality of the novel arises from the pace and the variety of the actions, the threads of which are woven together at the end. This unity is coyly suggested in the titles of the four sections of the book: "Priming the Canvas," "The Landscape," "Figuring the Foreground," and "The Varnish." In a novel about painting, these titles suggest the construction of a work of art. Each of the sections is introduced with an epigraph, a quote from a famous painter or commentator on art. These epigraphs at first seem fairly straightforward, but the subsequent events in the novel turn them into a somewhat ironic comment on the novel's concerns. For instance, the first epigraph, "One does not marry art. One ravishes it," is attributed to the nineteenth-century French painter Edgar Degas, and seems to be a comment on how a viewer appreciates paintings. But once the story gets going and the reader learns that the novel focuses on various people all intent on stealing paintings or cheating someone else in the buying or selling of paintings, the epigraph seems to suggest the original meaning of "ravish," which is to take something away by force. By the time the reader arrives at the last epigraph, "I know what it is like to be God," attributed to Pablo Picasso, it is no surprise that the quote is followed by the explanatory phrase, "dead painter," an ironic remark because "dead" is not a descriptor associated with God. The titles of the sections, comparing the novelist to a painter and to another "creator," are pushed into the light of irony, and the epigraph becomes a reflection on the aims of the novelist as well.

Character Development

Many of the characters in *The Modigliani Scandal* are plotters of one kind or another, thus making plot and character functions of each other. Even a very minor character in a remote Italian village takes great delight in playing a somewhat stupid trick on two of the main characters. The trick does not have a lot to do with anything; it just extends the novel's continuing and pervasive sense that shamming is the ordinary mode of life in the twentieth century and that people have to struggle to achieve authenticity in their lives. The two main characters, Delia Sleign and Mike Arnaz, come the closest to this authenticity, but even they have difficulty speaking directly to each other at a moment when each of them wants to make a deep and lasting commitment. Delia, an English student starting research for her doctoral thesis in art history on the connection between painting and drugs among some painters, is the character who initiates the search for the lost Modigliani that gives the novel its title. Mike, the American entrepreneur in international art circles, adds the business and practical savvy to develop the very elaborate scheme that finally draws in all the characters in the book.

Dee (Delia's nickname) sets the plot in motion with two trivial and innocent postcards, one to her uncle Charles Lampeth, an art dealer in London, and the other to her friend Samantha Winacre, a successful movie actress, about her good fortune at passing her exams with flying colors and her excitement at hunting down what might be a lost painting by the twentieth-century Italian painter Amedeo Modigliani. These events become the occasion for a complex adventure because Charles

Lampeth, ignoring any family loyalty he might owe to a niece, immediately hires a private detective named Lipsey to find the Modigliani before Dee does. The other postcard creates another treasure hunter when Julian Black, a would-be gallery owner, happens to visit Samantha and notice the note on the postcard.

Julian is an important character because his connections with other characters enable at least two other plot overlaps to occur and because his attempts to establish himself as an important dealer in the art world make him an interesting focus for the novel's thematic concerns. The novel introduces Julian as he approaches his wife, Sarah, for a loan to finish setting up an art gallery. Julian's thoughts reveal that he had started out training to be a painter until he realized that he had no talent, and so the gallery is a substitute for what he found out he could not do. His approach is full of dread because he has already borrowed a lot of money for the gallery from Sarah's very rich and titled father, Lord Cardwell. Sarah, an almost literal representative of "the idle rich," scorns Julian's request for money and taunts him about his sexual failures, thus echoing his lack of talent for art. Lord Cardwell, who has enlisted Charles Lampeth as his agent to sell his art collection, is more polite in his refusal to lend more money but no less condescending. It is on the heels of these disappointments that Julian sees the postcard at Samantha Winacre's house and begins to imagine the lost Modigliani as his way out of financial difficulty.

Some London artists comprise another group of important characters: Peter Usher, his wife, Anne, and Arthur Mitchell, who has been at art school with Peter. Peter is introduced to the reader as an artist who is just becoming recognized and whose paintings have started to sell for prices high enough to encourage him to buy a house and undertake mortgage payments. These financial burdens make it all the harder for him when the owner of his current gallery, Charles Lampeth, decides not to promote his work anymore. During a gallery party Peter screams at Charles about being ignored and very quickly finds himself in the position of the struggling artist, even if his struggle is with middle-class financial responsibilities. The novel enables its readers to find out exactly what Peter thinks about the art world and its pretensions when he interrupts the art class he is teaching that night to deliver a long tirade about art and money. Peter hurls all his rage and disappointment into a harangue against the commercialization of the artistic process that turns paintings into fashions and economic commodities while denying the artist's recognition and reward. His rancor includes all the members of the art market—patrons, dealers, critics, and viewers. From then on the reader is alerted to these specific issues surrounding the pursuit of artistic or financial success in the novel. Ethical concerns about art and money appear again in Samantha Winacre's musings about how her earnings as a movie star far exceed any ordinary measures of worth and make her connections with her working-class housekeeper absurd.

The last two major characters involved in driving the various strands of the plot are Samantha Winacre and Tom Copper, a figure who appears on the fringes of the art and monied worlds and is notable because of his presentation of himself as an authentic working-class person. The reader meets him first when he wins the interest of Samantha at a party and very quickly becomes a central part of her life. Part of his allure for Samantha is the drugs he offers her at that party and which he supplies to her in increasing amounts. Only belatedly do other characters recognize that he is not good for Samantha and that he is using her to set up a robbery of Lord Cardwell's paintings. Samantha's decline is likely to be distressing to the reader because early in the novel her reflections on the inequities created by the economic system created sympathy for her. She deplores a system that rewards her so highly for what she considers a limited investment on her part and requires others, such as the girl who keeps house for her, to sacrifice their own talents in a life of constant and difficult toil. She is generous financially toward her housekeeper and sincere in her effort to make her art have an impact on the world.

Plot Development

Because the actions of all the characters eventually intersect in one closely related group of events, it is important to remember that all the plot lines are significant even when one or another receives more attention and development. Dee's pursuit of the lost Modigliani, however, becomes the central plot line from which the others spin off. Another plot line, a literal "plot," or scheme, revolves around the fraud that Peter and Anne Usher and Arthur Mitchell contrive in order to revenge slights inflicted on them by various galleries and to teach the London art world about its own empty pretenses. Peter and Arthur decide to paint a series of forgeries of lost or lesser-known works by famous painters and then sell them to all the major galleries in London. This scheme mirrors the novel's intentions to reveal the foolishness of the London art world. The final major plot line focuses on a simple robbery scheme in which Tom

Copper reveals himself as nothing but a lower-class crook who wants to use Samantha's connections to steal Lord Cardwell's art collection.

The final plot twist is revealed at the end when Mike Arnaz explains to Dee that he has set up Peter Usher and Arthur Mitchell in their forgery adventure so that he can force them to make copies of the newly found Modigliani and expose the art world pretenders a second time. Thus, the Usher-Mitchell scheme is part of a more complex plot set in motion by Mike. Mike endears himself to Dee because the action shows a faith in her abilities to find the painting, and he manages to turn the greed and superficiality of the London art world to his own advantage and to their consternation. Mike ends up as the greatest impresario of them all; he is the one who deftly controls all the action on the canvas, or at least he controls the actions within the purview of the novelist.

Thematic Issues

Perhaps the overriding concern in *The Modigliani Scandal* is the ambiguity introduced when art is treated as merchandise. Follett plays with the contradictions implicit in the difference between what people ask of art and what they ask for it. The novel does not settle the matter, but the differences in the various meanings and values that surround the art world enable the author to be funny and flip about how art works and what it means for it to sell or not sell. He approaches these concerns within a larger framework of the purposes of both art and money. Samantha's comments early in the novel about how her money ought to lead to something good and positive in the world set up in the novel a major theme, which returns in many Follett novels. Her altruistic conviction is countered by Lord Cardwell's rejoinder at their dinner: "There was a time, you know, when I wanted to change the world, like you young people. I thought I might use my wealth to do somebody some good. But somehow, when you get involved in the business of actually surviving, holding companies together, satisfying shareholders—you lose interest in such grand schemes" (220). Cardwell's response to her idealism is no answer, of course, and the ability his wealth and position give him to deliver such fatuous responses sets him up as a foolish figure and so a ripe target for the various characters who show some sense and who scheme to grab some of his wealth. The disparity between the characters' approaches to money and the reader's perception that some are fools and some are clever schemers is partly responsible for the novel's comic tone. All the novel's tricks and plots suggest that the question about who has the proper perspective on life—the artists putting together a con or the con artists setting up a dodge so that they can steal something—is more complex and difficult than it should be. The novel's long parade of rich people playing tricks on one another undercuts the usual social expectation that people given extensive privileges act better than people without such privileges. The novel's comic turns bring the reader again and again to the suggestion that wealth and pretension aside, all people are equals in looking out for a quick way to pleasure and ease.

The novel's comic posture has another dimension that a reader is apt to notice and that Follett may have had in mind when he talked about the "serious intentions" that the critics missed. The novel raises a series of questions about how the impulses that create art conflict with the financial interests that art attracts, whether the pure motives and subjects of art reflect the actual lives and impulses of most people, and whether the worth and value art suggests can survive the economic forces so prominent in present-day life. For instance, the traditional analogy between the artist as creator and God as creator offers a sly comment on the silliness of the quote from Picasso. The structure and process of the novel are analogous to those of a painting, but the novel undercuts the significance of that structure and process when it reveals paintings to be fakes and strongly suggests that art cannot sustain the lofty claims and analogies that are often made in its name. Undercutting important claims about art or literature is common in late twentieth-century "postmodernist" works of art and criticism. Many of the critical approaches mentioned in this book take this postmodernist approach. A postmodernist is skeptical about making and sustaining large, global generalizations. Often postmodernist works use humor and irony to call attention to their own serious attempts to make sense out of life. These works do indeed intend to address matters of meaning *and* they insist on reminding the reader that generalizations such as these are risky. In *The Modigliani Scandal* Follett casts a postmodern eye on the world of art. He does similar things in some of his other novels, but he is also capable of making direct and serious attempts to develop meaning without the skeptical glance.

PAPER MONEY (1977)

Ken Follett has called *Paper Money* the "best of my unsuccessful books" (*Paper Money*, v). Like *The Modigliani Scandal*, he says, it lacks a central character but "features several groups of characters whose stories are linked and share a common climax" (v). In the reissue, Follett presents the book as a "caper" and so makes a distinction between it and his later books in terms of its tone. But while *The Modigliani Scandal*, also described in the reissues as a caper, has a light and jaunty tone and pace, *Paper Money* ends with a series of disturbing notes, although not quite to the degree of "almost a tragedy" that Follett suggests. The title calls special attention to the relative insubstantiality of paper money as a medium of exchange. The focus on paper, as distinct from commodities that have value in themselves, emphasizes the vulnerability of paper to corruption and subversion of what it stands for. This sense of the fragility of paper money extends to the newspaper business, high finance, and the dealings of the criminal underworld, all major settings of the plot, where in each situation the connection between paper, or any other symbol, and real worth or value is tested.

Paper Money places the reader in the middle of a series of schemes pursued by characters interested in increasing their wealth and power. The suddenness of the shifts from one character to another and the entanglements of schemes from one to the others create an increasingly hectic pace for the story. The structure of the novel keeps all the action within one day and so compresses the complicated activities. The fact that each character seems to be operating with pressing deadlines adds to the novel's air of urgency.

The story revolves around a conglomerate winning an important contract and the consequences of that action. It presents an ordinary situation with a relatively low level of conflict. What compels the reader's interest is the intense and complex personal investments characters make in the business-related schemes they have set in motion. In the world of the novel, meaning and value shift as people move from personal concerns to public actions. Defining elements such as loyalty, love, class privileges, and business acumen, which had controlled personal and public relations in the past, begin to take on different meaning under the pressure of the schemes at work in the novel. In the Introduction to the reissued *Paper Money*, Follett says he had hoped to focus on the threat to individual choice from institutionalized public concerns. His novel pushes that threat to a level that challenges traditional assumptions about how meaning is established and how values operate in changing times.

Point of View

This novel takes an omniscient point of view, in which the narrator knows all that is happening to all the characters and what they are thinking. The first line of the novel, "It was the luckiest night of Tim Fitzpeterson's life" (9), captures more of what Tim Fitzpeterson is thinking at that moment than what the reader will soon realize is actually the case. That distance between what the character thinks and what the reader sees through the eyes of the omniscient narrator keeps the story moving along with expectation. The folly and vanity of Tim Fitzpeterson is both ludicrous and touching: ludicrous because he harbors such unrealistic expectations for himself and touching because his failure to be realistic is a common human trait. The reader alternatively identifies and feels alienated from the characters, and this shift keeps the novel's point of view sharp and the reader alert to the nuances of character and action.

Character Development

Felix Laski, a shady, self-made financier, is distinguishable right away as a powerful and dangerous man because the narrator tells the reader that Laski uses pretensions, his and others', to get what he wants. His clear-eyed view of his life and actions contrasts sharply with the self-deceptions of many other characters and gives him a special position as almost a satirist, certainly a manipulator of the action in the novel, and perhaps a hero of sorts. It is Laski who develops and maintains a series of interlocking relationships with people to arrange the complex financial deals that have made him well known and somewhat respected in London. He strains his network of financial connections when he becomes involved with people at all levels of the social, economic, ethical, and cultural worlds. His role in the novel as the powerful manipulator of a wide variety of people and actions is threatened when the complexity of his expanded world overwhelms his operations. In the climax of the novel he comes close to losing control of his financial structures as he begins to fall in love, which is itself a relinquishing of isolation and separate identity. The excitement of characters juggling external and internal conflicts satisfies the reader's expectations of this somewhat comic caper.

Ellen Hamilton is another character who faces complex emotional decisions, but rather than participating directly in the financial and criminal actions of the novel, she has an impact on other characters. Ellen is the wife of Derek Hamilton, a corporate head who parlayed a successful, inherited printing company into a complex financial holding company that exhibits all the flair and daring of corporate conglomerates but finally loses money and is headed for bankruptcy. Ellen is like Laski in that she sees events clearly and wants people around her to face them squarely. She has lost respect for her husband and is frustrated by his failure to face the implications of his actions and by his preoccupation with the stress that is damaging his health. Partly in reaction to Derek's having let himself grow fat and physically repulsive, she has become Laski's lover, a partnership driven by lust and a mutual attraction to risk and adventure. Ellen's conflict between her loyalty to her husband and her attraction to Laski grows more complicated when both respond positively to her demands: Derek sells his business and Laski proposes marriage. After becoming convincing in the novel as a person ready to take strong measures to get what she wants, Ellen chooses to stay in her conventional life. Her reasons for this choice are announced but cannot be explained as a "caper." Readers likely to value both her strong character and conventional values might be unsettled by the lack of any reconciliation between the elements of her choice. Her choice challenges the reader to reestablish a sense of value and perspective in a novel where the connections between values and actions are problematical.

Tony Cox, the thug-turned-entrepreneur, commands a lot of the reader's attention and concern. Cox appears initially as the gangster who brings Fitzpeterson the news that he's been taken and that he must pay the blackmail with whatever information Cox wants, a painful price for a government minister whose job is perspicacity and confidentiality. Cox is clearly brutal and vindictive, but the reader is likely to recognize, and perhaps cheer for, the justification for his brutality in the initial chapter. Fitzpeterson had tried to use his superior class and education to condescend to Cox and so win some control over him. Cox's punch in the stomach is brutal, but in the context it is a fitting response to Fitzpeterson's posturing. The novel presents Cox as a thug, but that characterization grows complicated as he becomes the most successful manipulator among the characters in the novel and the most entrepreneurial of a group of people who make business and financial success their profession. Cox's lifestyle and habits appear as an only slightly skewed version of the respectable characters that inhabit the upper end of the socio-economic scale in the novel. These complicating factors may lead to the reader's consternation when Cox is caught up in the ripples of violence unleashed by his schemes. He suffers at the end, but how to locate that suffering in the world of the novel is what leads to the disconcerting note at the book's end.

Arthur Cole and Kevin Hart are older and younger newspaper reporters, respectively, and together they fill another character niche in the novel. They pursue the stories that the reader knows are afoot in London in the fashion that represents the best in the tradition of newspaper writing, journalists working as independent reporters and critics of society; but their efforts are complicated by the newspaper's corporate entanglements and their own complicity in the processes of corporate newspaper production. This conflict about their profession leads them to a perspective on the events that is both distanced and part of the complicity that seems to be spreading in the world of the novel. They enable the story to proceed, and they provide a sense of mystery and discovery that keeps the reader involved in the novel. The ambiguities that plague their work and force them at the end into a reluctant resignation remind the reader of his or her own frustration and fascination with the world of the novel.

Plot Development

In the Introduction to the reissue Follett talks about being as proud of his plotting in *Paper Money* as he is of his use of minor characters. He compares the rigid structure to the looser structure of *Eye of the Needle*. Limiting the action to one day unifies it and makes it emotionally compelling. Shifting from one two-hour period to another keeps the reader updated on the actions of the characters. Within each two-hour segment each of the plot lines moves forward with its scheme and closer to a convergence with the other plot lines. Although each character imagines that his or her own scheme is under control and headed toward success, the reader recognizes that the increasing number of overlaps among the schemes may lead to complications for the participants and inevitable disappointments for some. A plot that manages to keep its elements moving smoothly and ending happily, or at least appropriately, is a good read and leaves readers with a sense of a novel's accomplishment. But a novel like *Paper Money* lets its plot complications create too much pressure on value and propriety to make a well-knit ending feasible. It resolves its plot lines but most characters end up with something different from what they expected, some happily and others deeply disappointed.

The central action focuses on two heists: Felix Laski, the high-rolling crook, wants to buy up a major conglomerate at a cheap rate, and Tony Cox, the common thug with high-rolling pretensions, wants to pull off an armored-car theft. The personal lives and ambitions of the people caught up in these schemes complicate the reader's sense of these actions as mere crime stories. The increasing overlaps of these schemes create the dramatic tension of the possible consequences for characters as the schemes go forward, succeeding in some respects and failing miserably at others. The mixed endings of the schemes establish the ambivalent ending for the novel. Follett's thematic aims benefit from this ambivalence even if those readers expecting a usual crime-story ending are disappointed.

Thematic Issues

The "joke" of this somewhat comic caper is that important events in business, public policy, and the personal relationships of community leaders whom a reader might have expected to be honest and dedicated to truth and publicly recognized success, are, in fact, riddled with corruptions of one sort or another. The satiric perspective of Laski, the predator who rips away masks of pretension, invites the reader to enjoy these revelations but then leaves him or her with the need to find a way to account for these failings. But the novel does not offer a convenient framework within which follies and vices are judged and perhaps punished. Rather, the reader finds a world where vice and folly permeate everything, even the unmasker himself. The narrator reveals a story that ought to lead to a ringing condemnation of excesses and falsehoods, but instead it turns from one level and aspect of society to another and finds more of the same. The ending leaves the reader with a recognition that sometimes people do the decent thing and that sometimes the wicked suffer, but these consequences do not follow in any systematic fashion. The lack of differentiation among the sectors of the moral and social society of the novel, which at first seemed comic, finally makes the reader uneasy about the possibilities for goodness and trust in the world, and so the novel ends on what is perhaps an even gloomier note than the tragic suggestion Follett makes. At least in a tragedy somebody learns something or a wrong is expunged from the world. In *Paper Money* values prove as insubstantial and untrustworthy as paper money. In later novels Follett finds more cause for hope, but in 1977 he offers not much moral ease and satisfaction to his reader even as the author gets better at telling a good story.

ON WINGS OF EAGLES (1983)

The cover of *On Wings of Eagles* announces a feature that few best-selling adventure stories can claim: "With 16 Pages of Photos." The unique feature of this adventure story is that it is true and can thus present pictures of its real participants before, during, and after the event. It stays close to the facts and still presents the reader with a compelling adventure story. *On Wings of Eagles* tells the story of the rescue of two American employees of Electronic Data Systems (EDS) who were held captive by the Iranian government in the hectic months in late 1979 and early 1980 between the fall of the shah and the rise of the fundamentalist Islamic populist Ayatollah Khomeini as the leader of Iran. The rescue has all the elements of a fiction adventure: two good guys falsely accused and imprisoned in a country where political upheaval makes all its governmental processes arbitrary, capricious, and completely undependable; the failure of all the prisoners' own government's efforts to get them out; and the mobilization of a group of amateurs by a determined leader to pull off an amazing rescue. The book recounts the careful planning and the series of difficult and gutsy decisions that went into the rescue attempt. The rescue itself has enough surprises and moments of chilling tension to qualify as a thriller. And the run for the border through an increasingly dangerous and difficult countryside offers the thrill-a-minute action that is the stuff of novels and movies.

On Wings of Eagles is notable also because of the extraordinary nature of its chief character, Ross Perot. Perot represents the embodiment of the American dream. He started EDS with only some ideas and a lot of determination and built it into a worldwide business. He has since campaigned for the presidency of the United States and has inspired a group of followers dedicated to making his principles the guiding force in U.S. foreign and domestic policy. Perot's presence in the book drives all the other characters because he has demanded of his employees a commitment to the company and to the principles that run it. The rescue of the two employees in Iran succeeded only because Perot had built the kind of private empire that could develop an operation on a governmental scale. He could call upon his employees to pursue such a mission because he had made it company policy to recruit former military personnel. *On Wings of Eagles*, then, is believable as an adventure undertaken by a group of "minutemen" called into action by principle and commitment to freedom. The paradox at the heart of the book and of Perot's world is that the principles of freedom and American individuality are enshrined in a tightly controlled and organized company. For the purposes of the book, the conflict between the driving principles and the organization of EDS does not stand in the way of mounting an extraordinary and successful rescue operation.

Follett has high regard for the work he did in *On Wings of Eagles*. He learned a whole new way of writing novels through the techniques he had to devise for the book, especially as he addressed the biggest problem of how to explain the preliminary negotiations without losing the reader in the endless back-and-forth exchanges about small but important details. He solved it by using dialogue in the form of telephone calls between Perot and his operatives. Follett announces in the Preface that he has managed to keep the writing factual by recreating the conversations that he heard about in interviews and then submitting the drafts of the recreated conversations to the participants to check the authenticity of the drift, if not the actual words. He also did extensive research among the people involved in the rescue and in the published literature and public records on the period of the revolution in Iran.

Follett also worried about working with such a strong person as Perot. Perot wanted an authorized version of the rescue to be written before an unauthorized book appeared. Follett had been approached because Margot Perot, Perot's wife, liked Follett's writing. Follett found that he developed a good working relationship with Perot and with all the individuals involved. His Acknowledgments page recognizes many people and offers a special appreciation of Perot himself: "Finally I thank Ross Perot, without whose astonishing energy and determination not only this book, but the adventure that is its subject, would have been impossible" (413).

Follett developed a good bit of respect for Perot. When asked if Perot might have wanted *Wings* written to bolster his bid for political influence, Follett replied that he did not think that Perot operated through that kind of self-promotion. He offered the opinion that Perot wanted the accomplishments of the rescue presented because of Perot's deep respect and admiration for Colonel "Bull" Simmons, the retired military officer he persuaded to plan and lead the rescue. Follett suggests that Simmons, not Perot, is the hero of *Wings*. He points out that Perot himself is a great tale-teller, partly because of his gift for exaggeration. Follett was impressed with Perot's constant concern for the accuracy and precision of the story told in *Wings*. Follett was required to gather information, write it up, check the account with the participants, and then make the changes necessary to make it precise (Interview, 22 May 1995).

The epigraph to *On Wings of Eagles* might strike the reader as pushing the enthusiasm for Ross Perot and his team too hard. "I bore you on eagles' wings and brought you to myself" (Exodus 19:4) refers to God's protection of his people and his pledge to save them from affliction. The analogy between God's intervening in the trouble of the Israelites and Perot's mission to save his employees is parallel but certainly presumptuous. The choice of that epigraph, however, may have been driven not by pride, but by the nickname "eagle" that Perot uses for his employees. In describing Perot's regard for Jay Coburn and Pat Sculley, the two men he picked to direct the rescue operation, the narrator explains Perot's use of "eagle" as a criterion for measuring employees:

> Perot liked and trusted both men. They were what he called eagles: high-fliers, who used their initiative, got the job done, gave him results not excuses. The motto of EDS's recruiters was: Eagles Don't Flock—You Have to Find Them One at a Time. One of the secrets of Perot's business success was his policy of going looking for men like this, rather than waiting and hoping they would apply for a job. (85)

The spirit that drives EDS explains itself in these terms evoking fierce and rugged individualism. The independence that Perot shows in all his decisions suggests that the analogy to the biblical situation, if still somewhat uppity, does reflect the attitudes that permeate the rescuers and the actions that make up the book itself.

The book is successful in conveying all the ins and outs of planning a complex rescue operation, and Follett is successful in keeping the reader on board while these plans are being made. In addition to the phone-call narrative strategy mentioned earlier, Follett is careful to give the reader information on the worsening political and social situation in Tehran. The details about the mobs, the difficulty in driving from one part of the city to another, and even the details about the arrangements being made to evacuate American citizens add to the reader's sense of tension. As the planning proceeds, the sense of urgency builds and keeps the reader engaged. The balance between action racing toward a climax and pauses to sort through the elements of character and action keeps the reader involved in the people and makes this true story gripping and compelling.

On Wings of Eagles succeeds by infusing a huge amount of factual data and narrative accounts with the energy and imagination of a novelist who has already achieved outstanding success at writing thrillers. The achievement of the book arises from Follett's skill at accurately portraying the action in a fast-paced, engaging, and thrilling narrative. *On Wings of Eagles* deserves the status of a best-seller: It makes a thrilling read out of an exciting story from real life.

Genre

Ken Follett's first novels sold only a few thousand copies in a limited market. This inauspicious start convinced him that success meant writing good stories that would appeal to a wide audience. He achieved that success as he learned to write one specific kind of novel, the spy thriller. The novels that have earned the greatest success concern spies and intrigue. They catch their readers up in the suspense of who will win the struggle and how. Two of Follett's more recent novels, *The Pillars of Wisdom* and *A Dangerous Fortune*, use a different format, the family saga, to create stories no less compelling but in a significantly different way. In sagas the characters and their dynamics are as much the plot as the actions, and so the suspense and tension arise not from the excitement of a chase but from the mounting pressures within the family framework. Like any successful writer, Follett will continue to pursue those kinds of writing that best serve his talents and his interests. He may return to spy thrillers or he may write more sagas or he may look for a new form to capture his special vision of modern life. His latest novel, *A Place Called Freedom,* and in some respects his earlier *Night over Water*, add an element of traditional historical romance to the saga and suspense formats with extended chases and families in conflict with a hero. Follett has clearly moved beyond the thriller genre, but he brings the value of excitement and suspense with him.

Whatever interest a given reader may bring to a novel, it helps readers of a popular author to consider the impact *form* has on a particular book. The following consideration of the forms that Follett uses in his writing provides a framework for thinking about how and why these books are so successful. These concerns take their name from *genre*, the French word for "kind." It is common in literary discussions to examine genre, the kind of writing, to gain a sense of what to expect and to evaluate whether or not the book meets the norms of that kind of writing. Taking the time to think about how spy novels work in general enables readers to focus on what Follett does to make his spy thrillers so successful. Knowing the ways that sagas and historical romances work for other writers gives Follett readers a way to catch up with his new directions in writing.

HISTORY IN KEN FOLLETT'S NOVELS

Before turning to the generic characteristics of Follett's writing, it would be useful to take note of the role that history plays in several of them. While it is true that every story has to be set in some place and time, many novels make use of historical settings. Indeed, one of the major changes that Follett made from his early, unsuccessful novels was to focus on specific and important historical moments as the setting for the later novels. The early novels were adventure stories set in times and places contemporary with their writing; they almost might be set in any time or any place. But *Eye of the Needle* is located at a pivotal point in World War II, and the action of the novel is central to the outcome of the war. The Preface to *Eye* reminds the reader about the attempts made by Allied forces in early 1944 to convince the Germans that the Allies were amassing a huge army in southeastern England in preparation for an invasion on the Pas de Calais, thus diverting attention from Normandy, the actual target of the invasion. He mentions that the Germans suspected a trick and tried to discover the truth. Follett ends the Preface with a sly suggestion about the blurred border between factual history and plausible fiction, where, of course, the novel will exist: "It is known that the Germans saw the signs they were meant to see in East Anglia. It is also known that they suspected a trick, and that they tried very hard to discover the truth. . . . That much is history. What follows is fiction. . . . Still and all, one suspects something like this must have happened" (x). This imaginative fictional leap into history brings to the story a sense of importance, urgency, and veracity. An epigraph to the novel from the noted historian A.J.P. Taylor concerning Hitler's own intuitions about the pending Allied invasion strengthens that sense of historicity. Follett enlists history as a major player in this novel and makes it a built-in lure to engage the reader. Indeed, history is almost a character in many of his novels.

Of course, risks do accompany the advantages of situating a novel within a familiar historical event. Such placement requires that the writer portray details, as well as the larger picture, accurately. When he talks about his sagas, Follett stresses the extensive and careful research that must precede the writing. In an interview following the publication of *The Pillars of Wisdom* (1989), he explained that thirteen years earlier he had written the first seven thousand words of a novel about the building of a cathedral but had abandoned it because he "intuitively grasped that [he] didn't know enough about cathedrals or about writing novels." (Moritz, *Current Biography*, 35). Follett spent ten years reading up on the Middle Ages and visiting cathedrals before returning to the book about cathedrals and investing the three years and three months it took to write *Pillars.* Spy novels often do not need the same degree of accuracy because readers are not as familiar with the details of espionage in light of the fact that real spies necessarily keep their work secret. Nevertheless, the author must still keep the big historical framework accurate. The reader is likely to keep an eye out for convincing detail and so will be gratified by details that corroborate historical fact and frustrated by inaccuracies. Just as familiar settings in any novels create a mirror for values and assumptions not so easily recognizable in day-to-day life, so stories set in important historical events enable readers to examine issues and values. Thus history is a powerful and instrumental part of Ken Follett's success.

THE SPY THRILLER

Because spy stories are widely read and movies based on spy stories are even more widely seen, modern readers come to a novel with assumptions about spying based upon novels and movies (Cawelti and Rosenberg, *The Spy Story*, 15). In devoting most of his novelistic career to spy thrillers, Ken Follett taps into an already important market, but he also assumes the challenge of writing to an audience with very specific and well-honed expectations. The encounter between the spy and the hunter or the spy and the menace to civilization enacts for the reader some of the tensions and concerns that permeate modern life. The uncertainty that creates the tension in the novel exists at some level in daily life. The reader's rapt attention arises as much from apprehension about the state of the world as from the writer's narrative skill.

Perhaps the most prominent aspect of a thriller lies in its capacity to provide a thrill for every reader. That thrill arises from the threat posed to something the reader values. Especially when the reader identifies with the good and just cause here endangered, the sense of urgency provides constant excitement. That sense of identification with the cause at stake is a telling part of any novel. Readers want to follow the fortunes of characters they recognize as like themselves or at least as sharing their worldview. The dangerous and menacing characters show some willingness to deviate from the basic values inherent in that worldview, hence the danger and the threat. Readers begin to be tense about the behavior of villains when they sense that their security might be seriously threatened if people like the villains were to gain control of their world. The thrill of the reading is bound up with the sense of danger that one character, or set of characters, represents and the subsequent thrill of seeing that danger put to rest as the story plays out. What happens in between is, of course, the art of the novelist.

Suspense arises partially from the careful handling of details. In a sense, the reader helps to create the suspense by latching on to one detail or another and instantly projecting potential consequences. Often readers find thrillers wonderfully suspenseful even when they anticipate the final outcome. Even if the reader can project the outcome of the story, the details of exactly how that happens are in doubt, which casts doubt on the certainty about the ending and creates the suspense.

The novelist often will offer the reader inside information and so implicate the reader in the business of bringing the characters into the state of knowledge they need in order to succeed or in order to reveal their certain demise. This inside information acts as dramatic irony does in many kinds of literary works. Dramatic irony is a device that encourages a reader's involvement by giving some important information about a character that the character does not have. The reader's special perspective makes it possible to anticipate the upcoming problems before the character does and so the reader joins the writer in propelling the story to its anticipated end. The reader stays engrossed not so much to find out what happens, because, if the story follows its generic form, that part will be more or less predictable, as to make sure that what he or she expects to happen does in fact occur. Experience with detective novels might lead readers to believe that suspense is created by only a very few clues, but the successful thriller provides lots of clues. Take, for instance, the chase in a spy thriller, one of the most prominent devices in the genre. As the chase nears its end, the options are scarcer and the ability of the hunted to elude the closing circumstances seems all the more amazing and increases suspense.

This moment of closure for the reader brings together his or her investment in the working out of the plot, the satisfaction of the good read, and the resolution to the threat to the values or assumptions that have been threatened by the opening menace. The book creates a crisis, or expounds on an already existing historical crisis, which could affect the reader and the larger society that the reader inhabits, and then sets out the mechanisms for solving that crisis and putting to rest the threat to society; these mechanisms control the pace and direction of the novel. The control offered by the defining situation is usually not automatic or merely obvious, but it does offer a clear focus for the reader's investment of interest, time, and intellectual energy.

George N. Dove's *Suspense in the Formula Story* offers a valuable description of the structure of the suspense process that suggests how Ken Follett integrates suspense into his fiction. Dove delineates four phases or states of narration: cumulation, postponement, alternation, and potentiality.

Cumulation includes the clues and other details that shape readers' expectations. Good novels are like any other structures: they have an economy that insists that the piece work as efficiently as possible. The details and other specifics that a writer provides in the course of any novel should contribute to its overall purposes; the more each contributes, the better the novel. This process is even more true in suspense novels where the details ought to create and nurture the sense of suspense. These details are the clues, promises, questions, tensions, and leads that will have an impact on events. In *Eye of the Needle* Godliman uses his training as a historian to pick up on the details that identify the spy and then begin to render his activities more predictable. In *Triple* it is the competing spies who articulate the pattern of details that contribute to the execution of the plot. Sometimes these clues lead directly to the effects that bring about the next element of suspense, but at other times they are merely part of a group of often unrelated occurrences that lead to the important events of the novel.

It is important to keep in mind that each of these patterns gives a different feel to a book. In books where the details lead directly to the effect that the reader observes, the reader is apt to have a sense that the world of the novel is a fairly orderly place where acts in one place have consequences in another and the rules of the game are consistent and reliable. In other novels, connections between the clues and the effects are often less direct and depend upon often arbitrary events to make the important parts of the novel come together. These looser connections between causes and effects create a sense of a world that is interesting and lively but also undependable and somewhat arbitrary. Both patterns can give a reader a sense of suspense; the difference lies in the world-view each presents.

The moves that characters make and the events that the narrator describes present readers with a series of information bits, each of which creates an expectation about what will happen later in the novel. The constant presentation and redefinition of expectations prompt the reader to turn the pages of a suspense novel and quite naturally to scrutinize the details that come tumbling out. The writer's challenge is to keep the stream of details relevant and helpful without making the resulting events obvious or uninteresting. When a writer describes the background of the spy or the spy hunter, the reader should expect that somehow that background will play an important part in the resolution of the plot. In some novels, background information reveals the nature of a character or engages the reader's sympathies in one way or another. But in a spy novel, information ought to pertain directly to the most pressing issue: catching the spy or foiling the pursuer.

Thus, involving the reader in the plot is a central task of the suspense novel. But a writer needs to keep the reader at bay in order to make the story last long enough to give him or her a satisfactory experience. Postponement, Dove's second category, delays the resolution and keeps the reader waiting for the exact means by which the plot is to be resolved. It is already clear that the plot will be resolved and no doubt exists, after a few chapters, about which character will be the victor. But the writer's task is to create a series of very good reasons for postponement of the resolution and convincing complications to keep the story going. In *Lie Down with Lions* Jane Lampert waits on her decision to reveal her husband's traitorous actions because she thinks she may be able to salvage her marriage and family life once they are out of the arena of espionage. Her commitment to home-centered values plays an increasing role in the plot development, and so the delay in resolution makes sense to the reader. In a novel such as *The Man from St. Petersburg* (1982) the main action is held in abeyance while the assassin adjusts to his discoveries about the people close to his intended victim.

Indeed, complication is central to what Dove calls "alternation," his third phase of suspense. The two competing qualities mentioned previously constitute mutually exclusive categories—details that point the reader to a resolution as distinct from reasons for delay of the resolution. The successful suspense novel alternates plot devices that move toward a sure resolution of the story and complications that slow the arrival of the resolution. This alternation keeps the reader engaged, as long as the balance is maintained. The story does not need to offer an exact balance between the two aspects. For instance, every move toward resolution does not need to be followed immediately by an event that delays resolution; the reader's engagement determines how that balance is maintained. *Eye of the Needle* compresses alternation into the exciting final stages of the chase. The race between the two sides to reach the island to capture or rescue the spy competes with the almost idyllic blossoming of love between the spy and Lucy. As first David and then Lucy discover and oppose the spy, the balance shifts so that the island itself becomes a location of the chase. *The Key to Rebecca* (1980) develops an alternation between the focused and effective actions of the spy and his neurotic and almost self-destructive pursuit of personal desires and fears.

Cumulation, postponement, and alternation lead to the crisis, the moment when all the clues, information, true and false starts, reversals, and premonitions take on a coherent shape, which suggests how the story will end. The narrative pace speeds up at the crisis point, and a sense of strain, pulling the disparate threads of the suspense story together, often permeates the narration. Dove calls this concentration of the action and information "potentiality," the moment when all of the possibilities raised in the novel come together to shape the final action. The moment in *Eye of the Needle* when Lucy decides to attack the spy is a moment of potentiality moving into action. Even Follett's nonfictional *On Wings of Eagles* approximates the movement of a spy novel in its closing chapters as the final barriers to escape come down and the prisoners race toward safe territory in what is almost a free fall.

These four elements of suspense novels do not occur in their entirety in every novel, nor do they always occur in the same order. But most suspense novels have at least the following elements: a problem, the first analysis, complication, period of confusion, dawning light, solution, and the explanation (Dove, 78–85). The problem may involve a conflict of individuals or a conflict of an individual vs. a menace to civilization. (Some writers classify the one-on-one conflicts as "suspense" and the one vs. a huge menace as a "thriller.") The problem is introduced in a number of ways, but the most common are (1) the description of a seemingly ordinary event that has a nagging loose end, such as the unexplained killing of a corporal assigned to mundane duties at the beginning of *The Key to Rebecca*; (2) the presentation of an extraordinary event that demands explanation or some kind of response, such as the building of the atomic reactor in Egypt at the beginning of *Triple*; and (3) the conversation between two protagonists (or two antagonists) identifying a situation that has to be resolved before their operations can proceed, as happens at the beginning of *The Man from St. Petersburg*. Sometimes the conversation also provides the first analysis, but that usually comes from the main character, who, for one reason or another, arrives on the scene to consult about the event. Such a first analysis focuses the reader's attention on the mission of the novel, but if that initial analysis were truly accurate and precise, the novel's action would end very soon and the novel would offer no suspense. So, the first analysis is often followed, either sooner or later, by a complication that sends the reader into doubt, and the alternation between certainty and doubt becomes part of the reader's experience of the novel. Quickly following the doubt, a series of events occur that not only complicate the plot but also undermine the reader's sense that the novel or the leading figure can in fact successfully solve these mysteries. In order for the mystery to be solved, that period of confusion has to end with a clue or a turn in the thinking that brings a new theory or plan of action and so seems like a new light on a period of darkness. That dawning alerts the reader to the renewed possibility of success and presumably renews his or her eagerness to solve the problem. The solution is what every suspense novel must provide, because it would be unacceptable for a novel to raise all these questions and then fail to answer them. The solution may be presented in the action and then followed by an explanation, or it may be explained and the subsequent action may merely act out the logical extensions of that explanation. Often the explanation comes in the form of an epilogue, which ties together any loose ends and suggests any interesting implications of the solution to the problem. These elements show up in some fashion in most novels; how they are presented and manipulated by a given writer usually is a measure of how well he or she has succeeded.

John G. Cawelti and Bruce A. Rosenberg offer five plot types characteristic of most spy novels: (1) the spy goes over, (2) the big job, (3) the hero as victim, (4) journey into fear, and (5) to catch a spy. These types help the reader gain a handle on the genre. Writers such as Follett, who uses spy-thriller elements in his novels, often combine elements of these plots; knowing the general types enables a reader to recognize the variations developed by a particular writer. The first plot type, the spy goes over, places the spy in enemy territory where he or she always faces the danger of discovery as well as of failing to achieve the mission. The reader is given information that addresses both of these dangers and so is engaged and "suspended" on two counts. Indeed, the reader's tension about detection increases the eagerness to get on with the mission since its successful completion at least eliminates the worry about concealment. The remaining attempts of the spy to elude detection become a single, focused adventure story. The master spy in *Eye of the Needle* has been living in enemy territory for more than a year, so the reader is given a detailed look at how a spy avoids detection. Even when the spy's activities are uncovered, the pursuers do not know what their quarry looks like, and so concealment and discovery are constant elements in the novel. Alex Wolf, the spy responsible for the action of *The Key to Rebecca*, infiltrates a hostile territory, but his concealment problem is anomalous because the place now occupied by his enemy used to be his home. The dramatic first chapter of *Key* focuses on his efforts at infiltrating.

The second type, the big job, identifies the task as a single problem so important or monumental that getting to it is a major task, a task so complex and elusive that resolving it requires a series of complex and dangerous steps. The big job challenges the spy's endurance as well as inventiveness. Outwitting the other side and getting the big job done requires the spy to call upon a wide range of strengths and, in some cases, an array of clever devices. *Triple* is a clear example of the big job. The hero must steal a shipload of uranium and bring it to his home country without attracting any public notice. The race, and the chase, involves moving around three continents and dozens of cities. The building of the complex scheme becomes as fascinating as the execution of the theft itself.

The third type, the hero as victim, creates a hostile landscape by involving the hero unexpectedly in the task, as an accident or as a small part of a larger plot. So by definition the hero is caught in a strange and dangerous setting. The suspense for the reader lies in the timing of the hero's turn from victim to agent. Although *On Wings of Eagles* is nonfiction, Ross Perot and his employees engaged in the rescue mission come

closest to this type. Follett heroes are often called to their tasks from
other pursuits, but they are usually not victims-turned-agents as such.
Eddie Deakin, the engineer on the Pan American clipper in *Night over
Water*, is victimized by the antagonists, and he resists the trap, but the
plot allows no opportunity for him to turn his resistance into agency.

The fourth type, the journey into fear, turns the "big job" inside out
and develops variations on the other plots. The spy pursues an unknown
but clearly dangerous enemy, but he lacks the assurance that knowledge
of the enemy brings to the job. Without a clear sense of the enemy, the
spy is always in hostile territory and vulnerable to attack as soon as
detected. Without control over the shape and techniques of the chase,
the spy is as much victim as hero. Some novels of this type give the
reader more information than the spy has about the nature of the enemy,
while some limit the reader's knowledge to that of the spy. Either perspective can work; the reader just needs to get a sense of how close the
crucial danger points are. Although Follett's first three spy novels, as
well as *The Big Needle*, begin with spy missions that have elements of the
journey into fear, none of his stories follow this pattern exclusively.

The last plot type, to catch a spy, focuses on counterespionage and is
closely allied to detective novels. In these plots, spies seek to discover
spies in their own ranks or in their own environments. Follett's novels
often depict spies chasing other spies, but none of these plots is specifically a counterespionage plot in itself.

Within these general plot descriptions, readers can identify common
episodes that make up these plots. Cawelti and Rosenberg list twenty-
three such episodes, which can help to put a specific writer into perspective. Examples of these episodes in Ken Follett's novels follow:

- initial ennui: Faber (*Eye of the Needle*), William Vandam (*The
  Key to Rebecca*), and Stephen Walden (*The Man from St. Petersburg*)

- assassination (attempted assassination): *The Man from St. Petersburg*, *Lie Down with Lions*

- abduction: *The Key to Rebecca*, *Triple*

- close call: *Eye of the Needle*, *The Man from St. Petersburg*

- confrontation: *The Man from St. Petersburg*, *Lie Down with
  Lions*, *Triple*, *The Key to Rebecca*

- disguise: *Eye of the Needle*, *The Key to Rebecca*

- disguised encounter or confrontation: *The Key to Rebecca*
- narrow escape: *Eye of the Needle, Lie Down with Lions, The Man from St. Petersburg*
- chase: all Follett spy novels, *On Wings of Eagles, Night over Water, A Place Called Freedom*
- evasion: same as "chase"
- on the run: same as "chase"
- capture: *The Key to Rebecca, Lie Down with Lions, Night over Water*
- interrogation: *Triple, The Key to Rebecca*
- torture: *Triple*
- the drop: *Eye of the Needle*
- exchange: *Night over Water*
- the plant: *Eye of the Needle, Lie Down with Lions*
- planted misinformation: *The Key to Rebecca*
- doubling/turning an agent: *Triple*
- turnabout (the hunted becomes the hunter and vice versa): *Triple, Lie Down with Lions*
- betrayal: *Triple*
- counterspying: *Triple, Lie Down with Lions*
- the tag: *Eye of the Needle, Triple*

Most people who have read even a few spy stories or watched some spy movies are likely to recognize these episodes. Some appear more than once in a given novel. For instance, "initial ennui" and "assassination" typically show up only at the beginning of a novel; "on the run" usually appears in the middle of the story; and "capture" is usually associated with the end. But many of the others, such as "confrontation," "chase," or "narrow escape," show up in the middle, ending, and sometimes opening of the novel. Although "interrogation," "torture," "tag," and "doubling" usually occur well into a novel, Follett's *Triple* uses each of these in the first chapter as an entry to the main problem. The combinations and variations of these episodes within a given novel are limited only by the writer's imagination and interests.

The characters who inhabit spy novels might seem to be an obvious group: the spy, the opponent, the support people on either side, and the innocent bystanders. The spy-hero is often an amateur or a person re-cruited into the business only recently and only for the reasons of prin-ciple and conviction. The amateur status of the spy sidesteps the question of motives: with no professional or monetary gain in sight, the reader presumes that the spy does the very dangerous work out of conviction. This clarity of motive and dedication to duty enable the reader to make a clear and constant commitment to the spy-hero and so become engaged in the suspense of the novel as the questions about the job and the danger and the chances for success come tumbling off the pages. The reader is in the spy's corner, at least at the beginning. When the spy is a profes-sional, the novel often establishes a distance from ordinary professionals and suggests that the spy's participation in the agency or the cause is sparked by principles and beliefs above those of the ordinary spies. This distancing gives the spy a status equivalent to that of the amateur. When the novelist wants to bring the reader into a more ambiguous world in which right and wrong are not so nearly delineated, the spy may be distinguished not by different motives but by an unusual capacity for honest and direct judgment.

Spies necessarily spend a lot of time alone, but they often need help from assistants, confederates, and supervisors. These others may range from mere subordinates to close and almost equal co-workers. The close-ness among equals may translate into an intimate and loving relationship with one person or the deep bond of conviction and friendship within a group. The added element of emotional bonds, whether with an individ-ual or a group, complicates the spy's sense of mission and duty, espe-cially when one or more of these loved ones provides leverage for an enemy. The number and range of associates that the spy has depends upon the job being faced. Against a large and complex enemy, the spy needs material and intelligence support and, at times, reinforcements. A writer's decision to expand the circle of supporters around a hero or a spy usually entails some responsibility to engage that larger retinue in the elements of the plot.

The enemy is likely to be surrounded by a parallel group of people, although it is in the interests of the writer to identify the bonds that connect these people as made up of greed, power, neuroses, and cruelty. The enemy's group, developed as it is likely to be from base motives and evil tactics, may be less trustworthy and more capable of being turned or enticed into betrayal. As with the hero's side, the writer's de-cision to invest reader time and interest in the enemy brings with it an expectation that these supporters will figure individually in the development and completion of the plot.

Supporting characters appear to be bystanders at first but may take on larger roles as the novel develops, sometimes because they were in disguise earlier. Certainly Elene Fontana in *The Key to Rebecca* and Jane Lambert in *Lie Down with Lions* move from bystander characters to central players in the action. Stephen Walden moves from reluctant host to defender of home and nation in *The Man from St. Petersburg*. Suza Ashford in *Triple* makes a transformation from being an acquaintance of the hero to being the savior of his scheme. Other characters may take on greater significance in the novel because they have changed their beliefs or attitudes in response to events. The range of characters in a spy novel may seem easily recognizable; the pleasure in reading such novels is often a result of the flexibility and variety with which a writer creatively uses the standard cast of characters.

Spy novels and thrillers appeal to the reader's interest in the unknown (Grossvogel, *Mystery and Its Fictions*, 15). That unknown may be defined for some purposes in large philosophical terms and may focus on the difficulties surrounding any attempt to be clear and definitive about life and human nature and the rest of the complex questions that continue to fascinate and frustrate humans. The unknown is also, at times, not much more than the contrived difficulties of a puzzle. The puzzle-formula novel carries much less emotional risk than the novel that poses philosophical questions. If a reader does not grasp the answer to the puzzle, then not much personal commitment is lost. But failing to find the right answer or to proceed toward an answer to large philosophical questions might threaten deeply a person's sense of being. Most spy novels and thrillers operate at one or another spot along that range between puzzle and metaphysical problem, and they make different kinds of demands on their readers. Those who read a lot of spy stories or thrillers become sophisticated enough in the genre to make something of a puzzle out of any work of that type. Writers reaching for more of a reader's philosophical attention will be sure to depart from the formula of the genre to keep a reader guessing the next steps and engaged in the themes and issues of the novel.

THE SAGA

In 1989 Ken Follett surprised many of his fans by publishing *The Pillars of the Earth*, a long novel about the fortunes of one family over three generations during the lengthy construction of a cathedral in medieval England. The focus on the generations of the family identifies the book as a saga. In 1993 Follett published another saga, *A Dangerous Fortune*.

The term saga referred originally to a group of Icelandic poems and stories that dealt with a wide range of subjects including kings, families, legends, bishops, and clan histories of various kinds (Andersson, "The Icelandic Sagas," 148). The most famous sagas are the Icelandic poems, but sagas appear in Old Norse and Irish literatures as well. Among the Icelandic poems the sagas about kings and families seem to have attracted the most attention from succeeding generations; therefore, modern understanding of the word is limited for the most part to stories about families, especially their trials and troubles over generations. Sagas are different from heroic poems such as *Beowulf* in that sagas focus on the family rather than the exploits of an individual. The values that are emphasized are not the personal courage and bravery that are extolled in the heroic poems but the impulse toward reconciliation and the desire for peace that make one or another of the family members a leader and a savior or sustainer of the family or clan. The distinction between heroic stories and family adventures is important to keep in mind because the events that constitute the stories and involve the family members are in fact very often adventures and great deeds of the heroic type.

Sagas often focus on the conflicts created by one member of the family who is a troublemaker or an evildoer. Some sagas use the members of another family as the catalyst for the conflicts. This other family might be rivals in trade or leadership or just a family that has crossed paths with the central family. Thus, the action of sagas often seems like a history of a feud or a lingering hostility between two families. Usually, when one main character is a troublemaker or evildoer, that character is balanced by a high-minded and talented character who is likely to emerge as the leader of the family and its savior. But these conflicts rarely occur as the simple battles one might expect in a heroic setting. Rather, the conflict is often worked out as a collective response mounted by the family, and so the family is seen as both the reason and the means for saving and continuing itself. That the family continues is the mark of success in such stories.

Like heroic stories, sagas are often repositories of family histories and agents for passing along the family's values to succeeding generations. In this sense they act as conduct books and offer young members of the tribe instruction in its law and traditions. Sagas are often meant to be didactic and so are apt to dispense with the rigors of realistic details. These didactic characteristics can be seen in modern sagas such as the *Forsyte Saga*, a series of novels by John Galsworthy published between 1906 and 1929. In these novels Galsworthy explores the dynamics of how success in business and progress in civic and societal prominence create personal conflicts for people at the beginning of the twentieth century. The Strangers and Brothers series of novels by C. P. Snow published between 1935 and 1948 bear many of the characteristics of sagas. These novels follow the social, political, and cultural changes in England and Europe as they are reflected in and influence the lives of two brothers. Perhaps the most ambitious present-day saga is Edward Rutherford's *Sarum* (1987), which traces the fortunes of a family in and around Salisbury, England, from the Stone Age to modern times. The traits, both physical and mental, which distinguish these family members from the moment of their origins, become lessons in values and interests that build strong families and civilized nations.

The Pillars of Wisdom and *A Dangerous Fortune* use the saga to focus the reader's attention on how the large patterns of history shape the lives of individuals. The use of the family enables Follett to capture a wide range of connected issues and concerns. In these novels he looks at how early capitalism provided a defense against the absolute power of the church and the king (*Pillars*) and how late capitalism runs the risk of establishing a new tyranny in society and government (*Fortune*).

The family is the central unit engaging in conflicts in *The Pillars of Wisdom*. One generation of the Hamleigh family commits an injustice against a woman who fifteen years later marries into Tom the Builder's family, which then becomes involved in conflicts with the next generation of the Hamleighs. The Hamleighs also plot against a fellow aristocrat, whom they succeed in dispossessing, and the daughter of that victim marries into Tom the Builder's family. The family is always at the center of the novel's conflicts. Tom's work on cathedrals puts him in touch with the most important religious, economic, social, and political forces of the age, and the fortunes of his family embody the issues and values central to the Middle Ages and still important to modern readers.

Follett uses the dynastic activities within a family to create his story in *A Dangerous Fortune*. Four families figure prominently in this saga, but the most powerful concerns are played out among the Pilasters, a wealthy banking family in England in the mid-nineteenth century. Just as the entire family fortune is coextensive with the bank they own and manage, their values, attitudes, and struggles typify English life of that day. Bourgeois capitalism in all its forms stands for reality in the novel, and tracing the family and its fortunes enables the reader to see the issues and values at stake in the larger society. The saga makes it possible for Follett to contain his story and his examination of values within the same action.

THE HISTORICAL ROMANCE

Ken Follett has used history as an important element in the settings of his spy thrillers, but he approaches history in a different way in *A Place Called Freedom*. In this latest novel, history itself is part of the attraction. Readers, especially American readers, are likely to want to keep turning pages in this late eighteenth-century story because it touches upon many events and themes that are very important to our own sense of history. The interweaving of events and characters that led to the American Revolution invites readers to imagine themselves in close proximity to stories that echo the important and exotic myths about their national identity.

Kay Mussell's Preface to *Twentieth-Century Romance and Historical Writers* suggests that romance novels and historical novels are closely related, although the latter tend to be taken more seriously by critics. Mussell outlines the concerns of romances:

> Romances and gothics take place in a world in which love and domesticity are central to the protagonist's value system and in which conventional conflicts are often centered around the family, however adventurous a novel's plot may be. Suspense may derive from the exciting historical adventure of living in an age of turmoil; it may come from the titillation of the outrageous and horrifying; or it may result from the exquisite conflict between potential lovers. But whatever the ingredients of the individual plot or formula, all romantic novels share a concern with the details of women's personal lives, of mate selection and family formation, of problems be-

tween lovers, and of the impact of events—both public and private—upon domestic affairs. (vii-viii)

Many of Follett's novels contain some aspects of the concerns for women's lives and emotions, but in *Night over Water* and *A Place Called Freedom* these concerns are central and driving forces. Follett superimposes on an emotionally charged historical plot a distinctly romantic story within which the rise and fall of characters' romantic aspirations become compelling. Whether one character does or does not love another one becomes a matter of suspense in itself. Once the matter of love is established, then the suspense shifts to the union of the lovers and the consummation of the passion that has been growing chapter by chapter. Both the unfolding of the historical events and the development of the lovers' fortunes proceed along parallel courses and intertwine at points, but they often remain almost separate stories. Historical romances are incomplete unions between two genres; when they succeed, these novels offer two distinct elements that complement each other even as they take parallel paths.

Night over Water also uses historical romance as an organizing principle. Much of the tension in this novel is generated by the conflicts going on within the hearts of the main female characters. The reader's involvement is engaged regularly by the fluctuations in the emotions and commitments of women on the plane. Much of what will determine the outcome of events and the reader's satisfaction hinges on women's romantic aspirations or frustrations. *Night over Water* is not only a historical romance; it uses devices from sagas and thrillers as well. Furthermore, Follett's novels have focused on strong female characters so often that the interest in female experience in *Night* should not appear to arise solely from the genre. By including historical romance as one of the formative contexts of this novel, Follett continues his habit of experimenting with genres.

A Place Called Freedom clearly has the hallmarks of a historical novel; what adds the distinctly romance cast to it is the class difference between the lovers. Because Lizzie Hallim, the heroine, is an aristocrat, she has access to the power and privilege to affect the fortunes of the hero, Mack McAsh, a virtual serf at the beginning of the novel. The social and economic chasm between these two major characters prevents their direct pursuit of an attraction that develops early on. The realities of class differences in the eighteenth century make it clear that any change in their relationship will have to come from Lizzie, and so her responses to events and feelings about people become important events in the plot and create important aspects of the suspense. Thus the book marks another innovation in Follett's career.

Eye of the Needle
(1978)

Ken Follett's *Eye of the Needle* met with instant success and acclaim. Rod MacLeish, a prominent reviewer, called it "quite simply the best spy novel to come out of England in years" (*Contemporary Authors*, 150), and the Mystery Writers of America gave it their Edgar Allan Poe Award for 1978. The spy story focuses on the secret preparations by the Allies in World War II for the invasion of Normandy, especially their mock buildup of forces in southeast England to trick the Germans into thinking that the Allies would invade on the Pas de Calais. Henry Faber, a dangerous and very effective German spy planted in England in the late 1930s, discovers the Allies' ruse and makes a run for Scotland to rendezvous with a U-boat sent to bring him and his news personally back to Hitler in Germany. Very soon after Faber's discovery, a British counterintelligence unit led by Percival Godliman, a historian by profession, realizes that Faber has the secret, and they set off to catch him before he can leave the British Isles. The novel follows this exciting chase and its dramatic climax. The tightly constructed plot variously shifts its focus among Faber, Godliman, both the British and German high commands, and David and Lucy Rose, the inhabitants of a small island off the Scottish coast on which the final chapters take place. Follett's spy novel has been celebrated for its exciting action and interesting characters. It has sold well over 10 million copies since it was first published and continues to be regarded as one of Follett's best books.

POINT OF VIEW

Who is telling the story, or the narrative point of view, makes a big difference in *Eye of the Needle*. Readers need to know that they can trust the person telling the story to tell it as it really happened, or, if the narrator is part of the story being told, that his or her point of view does not stand in the way of the reader's independent judgment about what is going on. The narrative point of view in *Eye* is that of an omniscient narrator, who knows all the elements of the story, including the thoughts and feelings of the people involved. This narrator sometimes tells the reader about events from a perspective that lets him or her know all of what is happening at a given time; at other times the narrator tells the story from inside a character's mind. From this inside perspective the reader can see the thoughts and feelings of that character from moment to moment. Such access to the central characters is valuable. It gives the reader the feeling of being right on top of the action and immediately involved in the story.

Of course, this involvement means that the reader cannot also be on top of the rest of the action or immediately involved in the thoughts and feelings of other characters. Writers depicting complex actions need to make choices continually about how to provide access for the reader. In making those choices they need to keep in mind these multiple tasks: (1) develop interesting and believable characters, (2) keep the action going at an acceptable pace, (3) focus the action and the characters on matters that mean something to the readers, and (4) create a sense that the action has some importance and relevance for the reader. In order to keep control of all these varied tasks, writers often switch their handling of the point of view as the story needs it. A writer cannot make these switches too quickly or without some good reason, but finding that balance of interest and reasonableness is the central element in any writer's task. Good writers find the proper feel for when one or another point of view is most useful. Usually, the narrator creates a sense of trust in the reader, whose confidence makes it possible for the writer to receive the benefit of the doubt in questionable strategies.

Eye of the Needle actually begins before the first page of the novel. That is, it begins to draw the reader into the details and significance of the story with the Preface and the epigraph by A.J.P. Taylor, a famous historian. The Preface is the voice of the writer bringing the reader's attention to bear on the concerns of the English people with intelligence at the beginning of World War II and so prepares the reader for the story to come. The epigraph uses Taylor's words to set up the importance of the novel's action. These materials invite the reader to think about important aspects of the novel before the actual "once upon a time" begins. Thus, when the first chapter opens, the move to trust the narrator is an easy one. The first two chapters describe important characters both from the outside and from the inside as they begin to think about their immediate actions. This movement from the outside in and then back out again is the characteristic pattern of the narrative for this novel. In the third chapter the narrator speaks directly to the reader about the narrative position, inviting him or her to accept these storytelling techniques for the duration of the novel. From here on the narrator is acknowledged to be in charge of the story and becomes trustworthy.

The narration also gives the reader an inside view of German headquarters. This view places the novel's action in perspective and gives the reader an increased sense of the importance of the outcome of the chase. These shifts in perspective inform the reader that (1) Hitler trusts "the Needle" more than any other spy, (2) some German generals do not trust spies at all, (3) the infighting among the German generals might give the Allies an edge, and (4) "the Needle" is the most respected and the most independent of German spies. The narrative also skips to the British high command to establish the fact that Winston Churchill, the prime minister himself, has given the pursuit by Percival Godliman and his team the highest priority. These shifts place tremendous importance on the action and so increase the level of suspense for the reader.

CHARACTER DEVELOPMENT

Faber is recognizable from the beginning as a thoroughly professional spy. In the opening pages the narrator has strongly suggested that Faber is a spy, but the dangerous dimension of his character is revealed in a sudden burst of violence he unleashes on his unsuspecting landlady when she stumbles upon him sending a coded message. Like the landlady, the reader is shocked by the quick and deadly force Faber displays as well as by his cold and vicious dedication to his mission. Faber follows up on the murder immediately with businesslike reflections on his next step in covering up his deed and changing his habits to maintain his professional effectiveness. The reader is confronted right away with a scene establishing who the novel is dealing with and what is at stake with this master spy.

Faber exhibits all the requisite characteristics that the thriller genre demands of a spy: He is sophisticated and knowledgeable about even minor aspects of his job. We see in the first chapter that he knows enough anatomy to use his stiletto exactly and precisely as if it were a surgeon's knife. He leaves Mrs. Garten's house for another cover that he had already established and begins immediately to plan for his next dual-cover situation in order to carry out his mission. He is unflappable because he has planned for all contingencies; at the same time, he is quick to respond to surprises and emergencies with cunning and effectiveness. Faber maintains a low profile in his cover situations and is regarded by some of his superiors as the best spy in the field. Yet, he has a contempt for authority that seems to arise from his sense of his own importance, and he is noted among his peers for taking every occasion to insult and deride his superior officers. These are winning qualities in a spy character. Faber could, with a few changed details, as likely have been the spy the reader wants to win. While the novel follows Faber throughout, it maintains a delicate balance between presentation of his skill, intelligence, daring, and dedication and the recognition that he presents a serious danger to the values the reader holds dear.

The first few paragraphs spell out Faber's efficiency and professionalism in specific and relevant details that identify him as a focused and careful professional. Interspersed with these descriptive details are thoughts and perceptions that reveal him as a person. For instance, as he carefully prepares the corpse of Mrs. Garten to appear as an attempted rape and so disguise the nature of the killing, he thinks about her pathetic motives for trying to seduce him. This moment of sensitivity alerts the reader to the fact that Faber is not merely a professional spy but a person sensitive to the ironies and fickleness of life. A few paragraphs later he thinks that, although a careful medical examiner would recognize that the "rape" had never been attempted, he is not willing to carry the deception any further. Then he adds a snide comment about the German SS that disassociates him from those Nazi monsters and strengthens the reader's sense of him as a person independent enough to have an allegiance to his country and still recognize that the SS is a cruel and vicious organization in its policies and practices. Faber is clear and accurate about his own place in the war and has values that separate him in the reader's mind from the worst German forces.

A few sections toward the end of the chapter add enough elements to

Faber's personality to assure the reader that he is indeed enough of a person to warrant attention as a main character. But the narrator is careful to keep Faber at the distance necessary for an antagonist in a spy thriller. Early on in the novel Faber turns to thinking about his own personality in order to develop the rationale for his next identity and concludes quickly by offering the easy theory that he is single because of his work. His quick survey of his personality both reveals something and offers a reason why the reader need not look for more. It points out that Faber is normal and human in his absence of relationships. That is, he has the same sense of the importance of human relationships as most people, but this urge is subordinated to the demands of the job. If, as is likely, the reader is somewhat unwilling to accept this quick reasoning, Faber's wish to avoid any consideration of deeper reasons both confirms the reader's sense that often these deeper reasons exist and provides a rationale for postponing any exploration of those reasons. Such a postponement is important at this point in the novel because the writer cannot afford to let the reader sympathize with Faber's character.

The last few sentences of the chapter return to Faber the professional spy ready to continue on his mission. The description of his final arrangements of the room offers both evidence of his professional attention to detail and a slightly pathetic aspect of his personality: "Nor did he feel any sentiment about leaving the place that had been his home for two years; he never thought of it as home. He had never thought of anywhere as home" (12). The last sentence suggests a moment of pathos and another reason for the reader to entertain the theory that Faber is a complex person. That line of thought is cut short with a sentence that returns all the considerations of the room and Mrs. Garten to events in the life of a spy: "He would always think of this as the place where he had learned to bolt the door" (13). The chapter ends with Faber headed to a new identity, and the focus is back on his life and work as a spy. Faber has been introduced to the reader as an interesting and dangerous spy. In the framework of the spy thriller, this character meets reader expectations as one who is dangerous enough to sustain the action of a novel and one who might individuate the action enough to make the novel interesting and perhaps memorable.

In naming the character who will become the chief opponent to Faber, Follett asks a lot of his reader. "Percival Godliman" fairly begs to leap from the page of a medieval story that uses names to telegraph values. The fact that Godliman is a historian and an expert on the Middle Ages encourages interest about him as a version of one of King Arthur's knights or an instance of the "godly man." But Follett never pushes that suggestion so far that the novel slips from being a spy thriller into an allegory. Godliman does indeed have the characteristics needed to oppose the schemes of Faber, but Follett introduces those qualities through careful character development rather than by simple naming.

Godliman is first and foremost contrasted with Faber by the fact that he is an amateur pressed into service by the demands of the situation. The second chapter of Part 1 introduces Godliman as a dedicated historian researching an incident involving Henry II's travel back and forth across the English Channel in 1173. The opening descriptions of him show him so immersed in his research that he has to be reminded that he is meeting his friend Colonel Terry for lunch. At that lunch Terry reveals his work in army intelligence and asks Godliman, who had done reconnaissance work in World War I, to come back into the service to help him catch German spies in England. The text makes it clear that Godliman will certainly be a reluctant hero. His thoughts as he walks home after the lunch reveal his conflicts about going back into intelligence work:

> But the thought of leaving his work—and for how many years?—depressed him. He loved history and he had been totally absorbed in medieval England since the death of his wife ten years ago. He liked the unraveling of mysteries, the discovery of faint clues, the resolution of contradictions, the unmasking of lies and propaganda and myth. . . . Going back into the game depressed him, too. There were some things he liked about it: the importance of *little* things, the value of simply being clever, the meticulousness, the guesswork. But he hated the blackmail, the deceit, the desperation, and the way one always stabbed the enemy in the back. (18)

In short, Godliman is the complete amateur: He has all the tools for intelligence work, but he likes using them on questions of history. He knows what he is getting into and his memory of killing three enemy soldiers in the previous war tells the reader that he is capable of doing the job. An encounter in a bomb shelter with a crowd of brave and spirited fellow citizens convinces him to accept the assignment, and the reader knows that he is the hero needed to challenge Faber.

During the course of the novel, Godliman's basic character does not change, but he learns to pay more attention to the world around him.

He learns as well to depend on others and to value their experiences and perceptions in important matters. The power of the lone intelligence addressing complex problems, which has been such a successful approach for Godliman in his historical work, fails when he meets another lone and powerful intelligence in Faber. Although the two are parallel in many ways in the opening chapters, as the novel proceeds, Godliman shows that he has the ability to learn from and to respond to other people. As the spy in the hostile landscape, Faber, of course, has no occasion to open up to other people. Indeed, on the one occasion where he does ever so slightly, in his brief encounter with Lucy, the slight change in his usual reserve leads to his downfall.

Godliman's role is extended in the fourth chapter of Part 1 to include the person who will be his assistant and co-worker throughout the novel, Frederick Bloggs. Bloggs had been an investigator for Scotland Yard before joining the intelligence service, and in many ways he complements Godliman's strengths. Bloggs has been to school but not to university, and his is a practical and direct intelligence. He is the one who will wade through the reports and do the other mundane tasks necessary to pursue a spy as well as physically chase Faber across England and Scotland. Bloggs is a good solid citizen who is brave, dedicated, honest, and loving. He is devoted to his wife, Christine, who has won his heart through her regular and exceedingly brave duty as an ambulance driver in the Blitz and he is devastated later in the novel when she dies in the line of duty. Bloggs is almost eager to tell Godliman about her poor cooking so that he can go on to her brave actions, the source of his love and fascination for her. By the end of the chapter, Godliman and Bloggs have established a good working relationship. With that combination in place the novel has established the force that will contend with the spy, and the chapter closes with their conversation about a strange message picked up some months before and signed "Die Nadel."

The last central characters established in Part 1 are introduced suddenly and with self-consciousness on the part of the narrator for the purpose of building a story. The reader must keep all the elements in the story in mind as the novel proceeds: "Faber . . . Godliman . . . two-thirds of a triangle that one day would be crucially completed by the principals, David and Lucy Rose, of a ceremony proceeding at this moment in a small country church" (21). The chapter then enters into a narration of the idyllic and sentimental wedding between two well-born English people, one an officer in the Royal Air Force scheduled to fly his first mission in two days and the other his attractive and articulate bride.

The chapter fills in the background on their courtship and their prospects for a full and happy life and then sees them off in an open sports car on their honeymoon. The chapter ends suddenly with their head-on crash into an oncoming truck. Two chapters later the narration returns to David and Lucy and shows them as they begin a new life on a remote and windswept island as a retreat from the world owing to David's loss of his legs in the crash. The chapter reveals David to be bitter and emotionally scarred by his loss and unwilling to carry on any further intimate relationship with Lucy. The chapter presents Lucy as a strong and mature character as she resolves to be strong enough to survive on the island with her bitter husband and her infant son. The novel returns to this unhappy family only occasionally until the later stages of the novel's action, at which time they become central players in the story.

PLOT DEVELOPMENT

In the Introduction to the reissued *Paper Money*, Ken Follett compares the earlier novel's structure to that of *Eye of the Needle*:

> *Eye of the Needle* has an even more rigid structure [than *Paper Money*], although nobody to my knowledge ever noticed it: there are six parts, each with six chapters (except the last part, which has seven), the first chapter in each part dealing with the spy, the second with the spy catchers, and so on until the sixth, which always tells of the international military consequences of what has gone on before. (vi)

Readers may not notice the structure because the opening part lays out the elements of the plot so well that the repetition of the pattern in subsequent parts takes on a familiar and comfortable feel. As the events of the novel move quickly through a variety of settings and situations, the structure ensures that the focus stays on the central characters while the plot continues to develop.

Follett uses the first seven chapters, Part 1, to introduce the main players in what will be an extraordinary chase, the basic plot in many spy thrillers. This introduction goes inside the mind of each major character and shows the spy noticing Allied troops moving toward developing an expeditionary force, the event that the reader knows is the central concern of the novel. The pattern of alternating points of view within the chapters of Part 1 creates pauses in the intense action that relieve the extreme tension building up in the one-on-one battles here and in the rest of the novel and keep the story focused on the larger perspectives in the game of war as well as on the immediate conflicts. The shifting points of view keep the reader engaged and create a sense of the confusion and pressure of the chase.

Part 2 sets up the specific chase that will dominate the rest of the novel. The actual structure is almost symmetrical but not strictly an alternation. At the end of Part 2 Faber knows that he is to head north to a rendezvous with a German U-boat off the coast of Scotland at Aberdeen when he wants to leave England to carry his secret personally to Germany. The reader puts together the direction of Faber's rendezvous and the location of Storm Island, Lucy and David's home, and knows at the end of Part 2 how Lucy and David will fit into this action.

Part 3 sets up the first phases of the actual chase. The chase is marked by Godliman's feeling that he knows the spy, a feeling that occurs to a number of Follett heroes engaged in chases in novels such as *Triple* and *The Key to Rebecca*. Faber eventually remembers a meeting with Godliman while Faber was touring a cathedral where Godliman was lecturing. This new knowledge adds a dimension of interest as the hero and the spy come closer to one-on-one conflict and the reader grows more excited about an increasingly close and determined chase. Faber's memory of Godliman reminds him of his contempt for amateurs in the espionage game, which he had expressed earlier in the novel after he had killed the home guards. This emphasis on the distinction between amateur and professional is apt to appeal to the reader's general sympathy for amateurs, especially if Godliman may not be as ready as Faber for the upcoming struggle.

One aspect in Godliman's pursuit in Part 3 offers an insight into how Follett modulates the pace of the plot. Godliman and Bloggs follow Faber's trail to a small cottage occupied by two old women. Because Faber had killed previous people he had encountered on his run, the reader is ready for him to kill the women and is relieved when he lets them live. The break in the pattern enables the interaction with the women to become another of Follett's portraits of ordinary English people. The energy and pluck of these women suggest the value of the national character and so of Godliman's mission. The incident is part of the chase, but the focus on the details provides a pause from the frantic pace of the pursuit and a glance at the value concerns of the novel.

As Follett does in many instances, the beginning of the first chapter in Part 4 overlaps with an earlier chapter and shows the complex levels of understanding and perception that operate in spy novels. After Faber has collapsed at her door and she brings him inside, Lucy, quite understandably, begins to take off his wet clothes as part of her attempt to make him comfortable and warm. Faber, needing to hide his stiletto and the canisters of film, demurs and insists quietly that he will undress by himself. David and Lucy then talk about how unusually modest the shipwreck victim is while the reader, knowing how often Faber has killed people who discover his secrets, feels the tension that the near discovery creates. The complex levels of action—what David and Lucy perceive, Faber's presence in disguise, and the reader's knowledge—characterize the island chapters in Part 4. Those levels of action become more complex as Lucy covers up her sexual liaison with Faber and as David suspects him of being a spy and of seducing Lucy.

Part 4 offers a curious balance of the increased frenzy of the chase with the strange pause and peace of the cottage life. At the cottage, something like affection along with the sexual attraction develops between Lucy and Faber. Faber gives her some of the attention, respect, and interest that David has refused her for years, and she awakens in Faber feelings of the value and importance of intimacy. Faber's powers of observation and his sensitivity to subtle aspects of the interactions between Lucy and David remind the reader that the spy is a person of insight and intelligence. Their lovemaking is described in terms of gentleness and mutual satisfaction. Earlier in the chapter Faber happens upon Lucy undressed in the bathroom after bathing her son, and the narrator describes the encounter in terms that emphasize the innocent and genuine interest and trust between these two lonely people. This strange interlude of peace and innocent affection is contrasted to the storm outside and the increasing intensity of the chase.

Part 5 of *Eye* gets down to the business of the consequences of deception and the beginnings of the final struggle. The fight between Faber and David eliminates David and leaves Lucy as the only barrier between the spy and his escape. When Faber returns to Lucy's cottage, he satisfies her questions with a story about David staying over to help the shepherd, and the two of them go off to bed together. The reader is struck by the irony of this romantic interlude occurring as the level of violence and danger increase. The irony of Faber making love to the woman whose husband he has just killed is emphasized by the questions of Lucy's son, who asks them if Faber is taking his daddy's place. The reader notices the dual aspect of Faber, who is, at the same time, the cold-blooded killer who pushed David over the cliff and the love-struck puppy who seems to be developing a genuine love for Lucy, a person whom he must certainly abandon and probably kill. The various sides of Faber's character are juxtaposed in this section with chilling effect. The reader's fear of and fascination with Faber grows with these revelations. Although the increasing pace of the pursuit of Faber suggests that the spy's days, or hours, are numbered, the reader is encouraged to expect even greater levels of struggle from a character capable of such extraordinary behavior.

Part 6 of the novel opens up with a definition of the final stage of the pursuit. Lucy discovers the murders of David and Tom, the other inhabitant of the island, and resolves to escape from Faber. Once she does escape and sends a distress signal, the level of threat and immediate violence continues to increase with the close proximity of the two opponents. Intervening chapters indicate that Bloggs is bearing down on the island in a ship with reinforcements from planes and that the German U-boat is circling the island waiting for a signal from Faber. The struggle finally focuses on Faber and Lucy: he needs to get into the cottage to reach the radio, and she needs to defend herself and her son from him. Lucy's ability to outwit and finally to outfight Faber marks her as the heroine in the novel. Both Lucy and Faber combine attack and defense tactics at the cottage, thus making the fight not only exciting, but also suspenseful.

The fight at the cottage repeats the split between amateur and professional that has been a part of the novel since its opening. Lucy fires a shotgun for the first time in her life and then develops some skill in understanding what she needs to do to use it well. She becomes wily in securing the house and in countering the moves that Faber makes as he tries to get in. She reacts instinctively when she takes a swipe at his hand with an ax and then vomits at the sight of the two fingers she severed. As Faber's level of attack increases, so do her resolve and her increasing skill and inventiveness. She even faces down Faber when he gains the edge on her by taking her son and leveling a shotgun on her. Faber is so smitten with her beauty and her courage that he fails to shoot her, as his professional expertise tells him he should do. Lucy's courage, inventiveness, and intelligence come together when she shorts out the cottage's electricity, thus disabling the radio, by sticking her finger in an empty light socket. Faber is stunned by her courage even as he is pushed to a desperate run to the cliffs to catch the attention of the U-boat, which has surfaced offshore.

Although Lucy's defensive mission is accomplished when Faber leaves the cottage to meet the submarine, her actions become heroic when she chases him to the cliffs and prevents his escape by killing him. The novel is clear about her transition to the status of heroine by pointing out that, as she runs from the cottage after Faber, she blocks out the cries of her son. This final impulse to stop Faber and save the nation identifies Lucy as a hero of first rank. The rescue team led by Bloggs is amazed by her actions, and Bloggs exclaims, "God, what a woman" (331), a phrase that echoes Faber's earlier exclamation. The reader is not too surprised when the Epilogue, set in 1970, presents Bloggs and Lucy married and living out the dream of social, political, and domestic happiness that had been threatened by the force arrayed against Britain in World War II.

THEMATIC ISSUES

The major theme of *Eye of the Needle* is the defense of Britain's national freedom from German attempts at conquest during World War II. The defense of democratic traditions against Nazi aggression is a common theme in literature of that period. By setting his novel during World War II, Follett underscores these themes. Characters do not need to spend much time evaluating the merits of the struggle; it is a given that fighting for democracy is their primary task. In large and small ways—cooperating with the blackout, serving as Home Guards, and volunteering for active duty—the British people exemplified the spirit of resistance and commitment to democratic values.

The novel illustrates the theme of patriotism in the actions of its characters. Bloggs's account of Christine's brave work as an ambulance driver portrays absolute devotion and dogged pursuit of duty in the face of extreme danger. David, and then Lucy, spontaneously make this same commitment, which suggests that many otherwise ordinary citizens have the capacity for heroism when the fundamental values of freedom and democracy are threatened. The novel's focus on the commitments people make to the values that undergird their lives counters any tendency toward cynicism about war efforts that might otherwise arise in a novel about spies and their pursuers.

Eye presents a strong case for a definition of heroism as courageous and intelligent action arising spontaneously to a threat from outside. Christine, David, Lucy, Godliman, Bloggs, and even the hapless members of the Home Guard compel the reader's admiration and interest because they represent pure and immediate responses to the call of duty. Faber also exhibits courage and intelligence, but his actions are premeditated and part of a larger plan initiated by the aggressor. Faber does not become a hero to the reader although the reader respects his abilities and his power. At points the reader has some sympathy for Faber's independence from and resistance to the authoritarian German high command.

The celebration of independent and individual effort represents another theme in the novel. Faber appears in a good light when he shows contempt for his too rigid superiors. Godliman shows the same impatience with the stubbornness of bureaucratic organizations when he bypasses protocol to obtain what he needs to complete the chase. The struggle for authority on the U-boat between the political operative and the captain, and the subsequent revelation that the captain was right, suggests the value of individual intelligence and instincts over the unthinking imperatives of large organizations. According to the Taylor quote that starts the novel, even Hitler made a mistake by trusting the judgment of his generals instead of his own instincts.

A related theme is the loneliness and isolation of the intelligent professionals. Both Faber and Godliman are presented as attractive, productive individuals who have isolated themselves from ordinary human contact to do their work. The novel suggests that Faber's strong personality traits led him to prefer the control over his life that spying gave him and that Godliman threw himself into his work as a historian in response to his wife's death. This isolation and loneliness lend a romantic quality to each man, especially as each shows a capacity for responding to human relationships when the opportunity arises. The isolation acts as a barrier to the unattractive parts of their worlds even as it creates the worrisome possibility that each may have lost his individuality in the retreat into professionalism. Field Marshall Erwin Rommel is another character portrayed as intelligent and resourceful but betrayed by the insensitivity of large organizations.

The novel repeatedly reminds the reader how much any democratic society operates through trust and a sense of community. From the opening chapter and throughout the book, Faber succeeds at his mission because people do not suspect that anyone would act in such a brutal and cold-blooded way. Indeed, Godliman has trouble in his chase because he cannot overcome the trust and openness of his fellow citizens. The degree of suspicion and the precautions needed to resist spies such as

Faber would eliminate the fundamental openness of a democratic society. In the encounters between Faber and the British people, the novel
argues for trust and openness as central characteristics of a free, democratic society.

LITERARY DEVICES

The most prominent literary device in *Eye of the Needle* is the title itself.
It alludes both to the statement in the New Testament by Christ that "It
is easier for a camel to go through the eye of a needle than for someone
who is rich to enter the Kingdom of God" (Mark 10:25) and the conventional wisdom about the difficulty of finding a needle in a haystack.
Furthermore, for much of the novel, Faber is trying to get out of a kingdom, not in. This needle is dangerous because it is the stiletto that he
carries and uses often, of course, but also because he acts as a spy, that
is, his "eye" poses a threat. An exchange between two radio operators
at the end of Part 1 teases the reader about the meaning of the name
"needle" but leaves the matter up in the air. The novel uses allusion as
well in reference to other works such as the Barbara Cartland novel mentioned in the first chapter to characterize Mrs. Garten and the reference
to Tennessee Williams's *Cat on a Hot Tin Roof*. Beyond these prominent
allusions, however, the novel actually uses the device sparingly.

The analogy made in the opening chapter between Faber's legs and
the pistons of a railway engine represents the kind of analogies Ken
Follett uses. The slow and regular pacing of the pedaling Faber does on
his way home from work in the opening chapter suggests an analogy
that introduces a sense of regularity and ordinariness that characterizes
the outward life of the cover Faber is using at the beginning of the book:
"He steered his cycle into Archway Road and leaned forward a little to
take the uphill slope, his long legs pumping as tirelessly as the pistons
of a railway engine" (4). The ability to operate carefully, regularly, and
methodically, like a machine, makes Faber a very dangerous spy
throughout the whole novel. His careful and focused responses to his
world make him a danger at every turn. The other dimension of this
figure—the tremendous power of a railroad engine—explodes within a
few pages of the opening when Faber suddenly kills Mrs. Garten, his
amorous landlady, as she blunders into his room while he is transmitting
a radio message. The comparison helps the reader to visualize the action,
but it also conveys a sense of the quality of the action as well as other

aspects of the story. This analogy seems representative of the way Follett uses metaphors and similes. When the narrator compares the recognizability of a radio operator's style of telegraphy to a mother's handwriting on an envelope, the reader can see Follett's skillful use of simile, especially when contrasted to the dead simile on the next page—"About as much fun as a dead fish"—used to characterize an unappealing and cynical spy.

Follett uses parallel phrases to create ironic perspectives for the reader. When Godliman muses that he liked the puzzle aspects of the spy business but not the betrayals, which he refers to with the metaphor of stabbing someone in the back, the reader remembers that in the previous chapter Faber had literally stabbed someone in the back. Bloggs's exclamation about what a woman Lucy is echoes Faber's estimation of her.

A DECONSTRUCTIONIST APPROACH TO *EYE OF THE NEEDLE*

The word *deconstruction* reminds readers that works of literture, as well as other texts, are first of all constructions. Traditionally, critics have viewed the meaning of texts as finished and final. Successful literary works have an element of finality in that they create a sense of artistic accomplishment. But deconstruction encourages further discussion and consideration of a text even after experts and other authorities have declared its meaning fixed and final. In other words, deconstruction suggests further consideration of those statements that presume to fix meaning about a work and shows that passages of a literary text that seem to convey an almost absolute meaning can be read in an alternative way. Thus, deconstruction offers readers and critics who find the received versions of reality in works of art, or of meaning in a critical work, unsatisfying or incomplete, an alternative view. Deconstructing a text opens it up to continued discussion and encourages the exploration of new meanings.

It is not surprising that deconstruction has met with resistance. Since the time of Plato, readers and writers in the Western world have sought to use language, especially written language, to fix meaning. Generally, the deconstructionist asks language users to recognize that there is no absolute meaning in written or oral language. Deconstruction does not deny that language has meaning, just that it has absolute meaning.

A deconstructive approach can be applied easily to *Eye* because the action itself is focused on the illusory nature of appearances. The success of the Allied invasion of Normandy was to ride on the Germans' misperception of where the Allies would invade. The secret that Faber discovers and that could turn the tide of the war is the elaborate hoax that the Allies had set up in the area around East Anglia. The novel pauses at one point to recount the surprise of a farmer as he watched his bull charge what he thought was a tank but turns out to be merely one of the large, inflated mock tanks the Allies had assembled to look like an army preparing to invade at Calais. The lightness of the episode, including the bull's as well as the farmer's surprise, offers a different view of the business of war and advances the suggestion that perhaps war is no more than shadows and mirrors. The silliness of the illusionary army and the seriousness with which its sham must be protected create a sense of absurdity at odds with the book's straightforward patriotism.

Eye of the Needle offers a fine opportunity to examine how deconstruction enables readers to enrich their reading experiences. The section on thematic issues (see above) shows how the values and concerns of the novel create meaning out of the action. Occasional complexities, however, compel the reader to consider other versions of what these events might mean. For instance, the most basic value that readers of *Eye* must share with the writer and the characters is that nations must protect themselves in times of war and that every citizen has a duty to defend his nation to the death. This nationalism, however, is undercut in a number of places in the novel, and these competing allegiances encourage alternative interpretations of the novel. Each instance that finds citizens of warring countries cut from the same cloth argues against nationalism and undercuts the validity of war. Perhaps the most dramatic instance of this transnationalism in *Eye* is the attraction and nascent love between Lucy and Faber. Isolated on the island, these two people respond to each other in direct and admirable ways, suggesting that national enemies might be friends and lovers if only circumstances were different. Faber's encounters with other citizens of Britain, especially the canal lock attendant and the two older women, suggest that human nature is the same the world over. These encounters may appear to the reader to be just local color or an example of the sound values of the British people. But a deconstructionist might see these portaits in a different perspective, which lends itself to deconstruction of the text.

Other passages also offer new possibilities for meaning. For instance, the novel introduces Godliman by describing the project he is working on, a puzzle about Henry II whisking back and forth across the Channel in 1173 between his holdings in France and England. This passage calls attention to the present, another Channel crossing to happen in June 1944. Henry II ruled before England was a nation as we know it, thus putting nationalism into historical perspective. Godliman's name and the connection with Arthur and the knights of the Round Table remind the reader of an heroic age long before nationalism. Furthermore, Arthurian legends provided a sentimental background for the expansion of the British Empire in the nineteenth and twentieth centuries. That romanticized version of the past may undercut the endorsement of patriotism that the novel seems to expect from the reader. This alternative perspective does not exclude any one meaning; it expands the reader's sense of how *Eye of the Needle* creates meanings that make it worth reading and thinking about.

The suspense in *Eye* and the poignancy of the events it depicts remind the reader of how close the world came to being very different, as a result of war, and that the difference between one way of organizing the world and another may not be as great as some would have it. A deconstructionist approach allows the reader to see how absolutes of meaning in the novel unravel, as the tale unfolds, into alternative theories of meaning. Deconstructing *Eye of the Needle* does not destroy the novel or the reader's sense of its meaning. Rather, like a prism, it enables the reader to see complexities and refractions that enrich both meaning and the reader's understanding of the way the spy novel works.

Triple
(1979)

Ken Follett's novel *Triple* takes an exciting adventure one step further than *Eye*. In *Eye* there are two opposing forces, and the chase that develops sets the hunter after the hunted in continuous action until the story ends in a stirring and dramatic climax. *Triple* adds a challenge to the reader by increasing the number of hunters and hunted to three plus introducing an even greater number of international players and pressures in the background. The novel focuses on the Arab-Israeli conflict; the action begins a year after the 1967 Six Day War in which the Israelis inflicted a crushing defeat on the Egyptian aggressors. In the novel, in 1968 the Egyptians construct a nuclear reactor with the intention of developing atomic weapons. This action propels the Israelis to rush to develop their own atomic weapons before the Egyptians do. This race has the primary elements needed for a suspense story, but Follett complicates the conflict by involving a third party, the Palestinian guerrilla organization, Fedayeen, in the chase for the materials needed to build an atomic bomb.

The chase itself repeats some of the features of *Eye of the Needle*. The chase begins very early in the novel, and much of the action moves from one complication to another within an increasingly narrow sphere of operation. Like *Eye*, as the chase builds to a climax, the action focuses on the heroic acts of a woman. The hero, Nat Dickstein, like Godliman in *Eye*, leaves a satisfying civilian occupation to undertake a dangerous

espionage operation, thus qualifying as the amateur hero so often found
in thrillers. But the hero also resembles Faber, the intelligent and brutal
spy in *Eye*, in that he is capable of a sudden and explosive attack when
provoked and proves to be extraordinarily resourceful in evading the
hunters chasing him.

Again, Follett sets his thriller in the middle of a historically significant
event and positions his hero to affect the outcome of turning points in
history. Follett does not need to suggest that the events depicted in the
novel actually occurred; just the possibility that they might have makes
it interesting for the reader to accept the story as plausible, at least for
the duration of the reading.

POINT OF VIEW

The opening of the Prologue places the reader suddenly in the middle
of an action that he or she cannot possibly recognize. The first line of
the novel, "There was a time, just once, when they were all together,"
propels the reader into the story because the sentence uses a relative
pronoun, "they," which requires an antecedent that cannot be identified
at that point. So the reader pushes on quickly to learn what the first
sentence means. The next two sentences do more of the same, thus compounding anticipation even further: "They met many years ago, when
they were young, before all *this* happened; but the meeting cast shadows
far across the decades"(1). The relative pronouns proliferate and the
reader is led to believe that paying close attention to this opening chapter
will help him or her follow the action of the novel. The subsequent incidents ought to become pivotal to the overall action of the novel, and
as events turn out, the promise is fulfilled in a number of ways. This
delaying strategy, which at first might seem like a pointless tease, suggests that the writer has full control of plot mechanics. The novel's use
of an omniscient narrator who sees into the minds of the main characters
assures the reader that someone has command of the story, an especially
important element in a story that makes a three-sided appeal to values
and sympathies. For instance, toward the end of the novel as the chase
becomes especially close and desperate, the narrator reveals a crucial
piece of information about who did and did not hear a specific radio
signal. Although the narrative for the most part alternates from one character's consciousness to another's, the narrator reverts briefly to the omniscient perspective in order to clarify where the chase stands after the

very crucial radio message is sent. Thus, the narrator takes charge in order to move an important aspect of plot forward efficiently and so fill the role expected of a narrator.

The omniscient narrator offers insights not available to the characters but also the perspectives of various characters. Some early chapters come entirely from one character's point of view, especially the chapters in which Nat Dickstein receives his assignment and initiates his plans. But, as the plot becomes more complex and requires the reader to know more about events occurring simultaneously, the points of view multiply to five or six per chapter, and at times the perspective shifts back and forth in a single conversation.

This ability to move back and forth within the minds of characters gives Follett the opportunity to portray the ideas and perspectives of several interesting minor figures. Minor characters do not usually receive much attention, but writers sometimes use their thoughts and feelings, as well as their speech and actions, to pass along information about setting, values, and attitudes pertinent to the novel's themes or to provide ironic views on events surrounding major characters.

CHARACTER DEVELOPMENT

The major character in *Triple* is Nat Dickstein, the Israeli agent and kibbutz resident whose mission it is to steal fissionable material for Israel. The reader first meets Dickstein in the Prologue, which looks back to the time "when they were all together" (1). At that point, Dickstein is twenty-two, a veteran of World War II and the German concentration camps, who is at Oxford studying Semitic languages. The gratitude that Al Cortone, an army buddy visiting him in Oxford, expresses for Dickstein's saving his life during the war conveys to the reader that Dickstein is a hero and a brave and resourceful fighter. Dickstein's quiet and humble response to such praise tells the reader that Dickstein is sure of himself and clear about his priorities in life. His reluctance to spend much time trading war stories, and especially discussing his time in German concentration camps, adds some mystery to him. But other characters speculate about his experience in the camps, which heightens the reader's curiosity about what happened and the effects on Dickstein. The interest in that telling builds from the beginning of the novel, and when Dickstein does tell someone about it, the reader not only gets to satisfy his curiosity but also notices that the telling of the much-awaited story signifies something special about the person to whom Dickstein tells it. This treatment of Dickstein elevates him to the status of hero and surrounds him with an aura of mystery. Although the reader comes to know Dickstein, he or she is more interested in the details that the novelist withholds.

The Prologue, set in 1947, presents Dickstein as an energetic, committed individual who holds strong convictions and beliefs and who is forward and honest about them. At the afternoon party at Professor Ashford's house, the scene of the Prologue, Dickstein enters a discussion about the proposed founding of the state of Israel in Palestine, the territory that Britain at that time controlled. He discusses the matter with Yasif Hassan, a Palestinian who would be displaced by the establishment of a Jewish state, and in the course of the discussion, Dickstein announces what becomes an important part of his motivation throughout the novel: "Never mind justice. I want a place to call my own" (9). This drive to have a home arises, the reader finds out later in the novel, from the insecurity of his childhood in prewar London during the heyday of the British Fascist movement, including Fascist marches through London at night attacking the homes of Jews, blacks, and others they hated. Dickstein encounters the anti-Semitism of the German concentration camps and so knows much about the vulnerability of strangers and wanderers. The first chapter presents him in his "home" on a kibbutz in Israel in 1968, where he cares for an orphaned child and has a good relationship with other members of the kibbutz. The chapter is careful to note that a young woman who works with Dickstein is very much interested in him, but he seems unreachable, perhaps untouchable. So his need to have a place to call his own is only half met in the kibbutz. He has a homeland but he does not call it home. He has no family or close relationships of his own.

Dickstein's character is notable in another respect: the novel emphasizes his position as an amateur in a world of professionals. Indeed, Dickstein's portrayal approximates almost exactly that of Cincinnatus, the prototype in Western civilization for the citizen-soldier. According to the Roman historian Livy, as Cincinnatus was out plowing his fields, the Roman senators came to him and asked him to lead the fight against the Aequinians, the inhabitants of a rival city-state. Cincinnatus left his plow and accepted the call. The story is famous because it has been used so often as a model for civic duty. Dickstein has just finished working in the fields all day when Pierre Borg, his contact with Mossad, the Israeli intelligence service, appears and Dickstein immediately gets up to go with him. Dickstein is the kind of reluctant spy so endearing to readers of spy thrillers.

Like Dickstein, Yasif Hassan is driven by a conviction shaped by loss. Hassan's deprivation comes with the partition of Palestine into the new state of Israel with other small sections going to Jordan and Egypt. By 1968, Hassan feels bitter about his subservient position in Egyptian intelligence and alienated because he has to work at a bank in Luxembourg as a way to support himself and cover his occasional and minor intelligence work. His bitterness about his loss of status and privilege hardens into a dedication to the Palestinian cause as he thinks about his parents being forced to live in a refugee camp. He parallels Dickstein as a victim setting out for revenge. The reader is likely to sympathize with Hassan's losses and the injustices he has encountered, but his petty, self-centered responses to his circumstances elicit very little sympathy, finally, and make him a fitting enemy for Dickstein, whom the reader comes to admire and like. Hassan is an interesting character because he is both a professional and an amateur spy. He is a professional in the Egyptian intelligence network, but since he is not a very good spy, he is given relatively unimportant tasks. Only a chance sighting of Dickstein, which makes him the only one who can identify the man, puts him on the team tracking the Israeli. But his decision to involve the Fedayeen is a voluntary action that he does out of conviction and so he becomes the amateur spy as well.

The third of the major characters, David Rostov, is also introduced at the sherry party in Oxford. He is an intense and serious ideologue who is quick to argue about values and political causes. An excellent chess player and a major chess rival of Dickstein, he remains Dickstein's rival throughout the novel, if, ultimately, not his match. Comparisons are drawn between Dickstein and Rostov throughout the book. When the reader meets Dickstein on the kibbutz, he is living the life of a socialist, working for the common good and finding what satisfaction he can in the progress of the many. Rostov, an avowed socialist, lives and works in the Soviet Union, but his life and aspirations are those of a capitalist, at least those of a Western materialist. He seeks ultimately to rise in the hierarchy of the KGB so he can gain the material comforts that are the prizes for success in the Soviet Union. He allows one son to pursue a taste for rock and roll even though Rostov hates the sound of it, and he wants more than anything else for his other son to get into the best school in the country, both middle-class, bourgeois attitudes. Rostov may appear to be like Dickstein, but important differences put the former in an ambiguous and suspicious light. If Dickstein and Hassan are people who have suffered from the forces of history, Rostov has been blessed by history. He lives his convictions in the country and under the system that he supports. The failure of that system to bring him happiness is measured by the petty, nasty agency politics that he plays and works at. He strives to increase his power in the KGB and by 1968 he seems to have forgotten his convictions.

Rostov parallels Dickstein and Hassan in many ways. His character represents the third part of the complex plot that gives the novel its title. But Rostov, although his aspirations and values may mirror those of many readers of *Triple*, ultimately fails to win their sympathy or admiration because he has no concerns other than his personal gain and comfort. Having lost sight of the grand purposes of his mission, he appears smaller and meaner than Dickstein and so ends up, like Hassan, as a character whom the reader is willing to see defeated. The differences between Dickstein and Rostov are apparent in the way they treat the Euratom employee who has information both men need. Both exploit the man's vulnerable personal situation, but Dickstein is honest and keeps the pressure at the distance of professional interest. Rostov, by contrast, pressures the man and his lover without any consideration of them as people and with no compassion at all. Rostov leaves them in the hands of Nik Bunin, the brutal bully who works for him.

Rostov never reaches the close connection between belief and action that readers want from the characters in an adventure story. He never becomes a full character because he has abandoned part of himself that is still alive and well in characters such as Dickstein. Both men exhibit an extraordinary independence from the upper-echelon people who direct them, and the reader admires that individualism. Dickstein's independence grows out of both his personality and his sense of effectiveness in his mission. Rostov asserts an independent position only after he finds that the bureaucracy is not working for him, so he goes outside the established channels to beat the system at its own game. That decision makes him interesting to the reader but not endearing.

Suza Ashford, the other main character in the novel, is the daughter of Eila Ashford, the Palestinian wife of Dickstein's main professor at Oxford; Dickstein had fallen in love with Eila in 1947. He meets Suza when he returns to Oxford in 1968 and is struck by the woman whom he had previously known only as a little girl. Similarly, Suza takes an interest in Dickstein and pursues him. Their mutual attraction and their lovemaking bring about a profound change in Dickstein. He tells her (and therefore the reader) more about himself and his experiences than anyone else hears, and in those intimate revelations the reader perceives Suza as an honest and direct person who makes and keeps important commitments. Her attachment to Dickstein inadvertently involves her in the plot, and she plays a major role in the ending. Many parts of the story are told from Suza's point of view, and at times, her activity and her perspective are the main plot interests.

PLOT DEVELOPMENT

The plot of *Triple* begins with the very recognizable thriller chase and pushes the action to make the chase even more exciting and tension filled than a usual chase. Dickstein is asked to go into hostile territory and achieve a difficult, nearly impossible mission. This assignment creates excitement because he faces exposure at any moment, and the reader follows the action with anticipation and anxiety about his being caught. Dickstein develops a bold plan for achieving the goal. The complexity of the plan, which the reader could not have imagined before the fact, and its boldness create the sense of excitement that drives the novel. Compounding the sense of urgency is the time pressure that the Israeli agents are under to obtain the fissionable material and build the bomb before their enemies do, even though the enemies have a distinct head start.

But even at the moment when the plan is forming in Dickstein's mind and the reader is getting a sense of its complexity and boldness, Follett complicates the plot by introducing Hassan, who recognizes Dickstein and reports the sighting to his Egyptian superiors. Thus, the spy's greatest defense against discovery in the hostile landscape is lost and the action becomes an explicit chase. The remaining action depends upon Dickstein's staying one step ahead of his pursuers. The shifting point of view keeps the reader moving from the pursued to his pursuers. As the novel proceeds, the shifts in narrative points of view within each chapter increase significantly so that by the end, a single chapter contains six or seven points of view. These shifts reflect and drive the increasingly complex and exciting action even as the elements of the plot become more streamlined. The intensity and the suspense increase because so much hangs upon so little.

The plot structure of *Triple* shapes the reader's sense of the importance of the various parts and persons involved. The Prologue stands apart from the rest of the action in time and in its narrative stance, as noted above. This preview of the novel's main players and the kinds of relationships that will drive the action alerts the reader to pay close attention to the action that is to follow. Follett opens a number of his novels with a focus on characters in conflict at a time earlier than the setting of the novel's primary action. The opening chapters of *The Pillars of the Earth* and *A Dangerous Fortune* work in exactly this fashion.

The first chapter also stands in an important structural relation to the rest of the novel. The opening narrative describing the attempts of an Israeli agent, Towfik, to shadow a German scientist in Cairo spends too much time on the step-by-step movements of the characters for it to be only an introduction to the problem that faces Dickstein. Other spy novels handle the explanation of the problem facing the spy in the opening conversation between the spy and his control. But *Triple*'s detailed first chapter has a special function because it introduces the reader immediately to the cruel and complex world of international politics and espionage in the Middle East. The deliberately graphic torture and death of Towfik is more pain and agony earlier in a story than readers usually expect. The added revelation that Towfik's interrogator and killer is a double agent working for Israel creates the effect of complexity. The introductions to the webs of deceit and double-dealing that comprise the world of the novel underline the seriousness of Dickstein's mission and the possible risks and difficulties he will face in carrying it out. The early chapters shape the reader's expectations and attitudes. The turn from the violent and disturbing revelations of the first chapter to the sunny and peaceful work Dickstein is doing in the wine vineyards in Israel suggests to the reader the alternative worlds of the novel and the serious stakes at issue.

The increasingly frantic action of the chase stops from time to time for interludes focusing on peaceful and loving ways to live life. The most dramatic of these interludes is Dickstein's love affair with Suza Ashford. He has gone to Oxford on a fact-finding mission, but his meeting with Suza takes him away from his schedule and creates an important change in him. He is struck by Suza at first because she so much resembles her mother, and he then responds positively to her interest and finds himself in love after they have dinner and spend the night together. He is changed by this encounter because this emotional attachment is the first personal and loving thing he has done in his adult life. The concentration camp experiences and his shock at discovering Eila Ashford's promiscuity seem to have stunted his ability to love. The connection with Suza awakens in him the feelings that have been denied for so long. Dickstein's control, Pierre Borg, becomes alarmed at how changed Dickstein is and worries about his reliability because his icy indifference to danger and death has been an essential strength in his work as an agent. Dickstein himself notices the change when he begins to think of his own safety as a consideration now that he has something to look forward to and someone to care for.

The action pauses when Dickstein writes a love letter to Suza from Germany. The action pauses again when he suddenly takes Mr. Cohen, a broker whose cooperation is needed to make Dickstein's plan work, to Jerusalem to meet the prime minister, Cohen's price for his cooperation. The trip is surprising and suggestive of Dickstein's independent way of operating, and it also creates an alternative rhythm for the plot as it halts to focus attention on a lighter aspect of the world of the novel. The reader is charmed by this aspect of Dickstein that can appeal to the dreams of people he deals with and with his impromptu inventiveness in carrying out his otherwise serious and danger-filled mission. The reader has seen Dickstein be severe and unrelenting in the case of the Euratom employee, and it is refreshing to see the variety of approaches he takes in putting the hijacking scheme together. The fact that all the while Rostov and Hassan are pursuing him constantly is in the background and no less real, but the pace and feel of the novel are altered by the use of these engaging interludes.

The romantic interlude with Dickstein and Suza early in the novel is balanced by another inset adventure at the end as Dickstein takes a small boat by himself over very rough seas to rescue Suza from the ship, *Karla*, where she has been forced to accompany Rostov on a high-seas chase. Dickstein's almost swashbuckling rescue is dramatized by the fact that Suza's presence on the ship with the Russian corroborates what Borg had told him about her being an Arab spy. But love wins out and Dickstein makes the dash to save her because he loves her. He decides, for no clear reason, that she would never betray him. His rescue of Suza also enables him to face his pursuer and beat Rostov one-on-one as he has Hassan and as his history as Rostov's chess partner might have demanded. Climbing aboard the *Karla* also enables him to hurl the grenade that disables her and makes her go under, thus eliminating the risk to the *Coparelli*, his ship, and leaving a clear course to bringing the fissionable material home to Israel with all of Borg's conditions met. The action ends with an extraordinarily exciting battle, a rescue of the injured heroine, and the mission completed.

Suza's character is notable also because of the prominent role given to a woman in making the success of the venture possible. It is Suza who outwits the *Karla*'s radio operator and sends the message warning Dickstein, even though she risks her own position on the ship and her credibility with him. She then descends into the engine room and overpowers an engineer with a wrench to reach the engine to disable it. Thus, Follett leaves the last and crucial actions of the plot in the hands of a brave and inventive woman. She demonstrates all the qualities traditionally reserved for male heroes and does what she needs to do to thwart the actions of her enemy. This pattern repeats what Follett did in *Eye of the Needle* and anticipates later novels such as *Lie Down with Lions*. Thus he has established himself as an unusual writer of thrillers in his willingness to spotlight the role of women.

The Epilogue moves the action ahead to the events of Dickstein's marriage to Suza and the roles in the Yom Kippur War with Egypt in 1973 played by him and by Rostov, who apparently survived the sinking of the *Karla*. The Epilogue shows the Israeli government taking care of all the loose ends that Dickstein had left as the last parts of the plan, and it suggests that Israel's possession of the bomb is what enabled Israel to enlist American aid in the 1973 war and convince the Egyptian leaders to sue for peace and so take the biggest step toward establishing peace in the Middle East up to that point. Published in 1979, *Triple* addresses the events that made news during that year when Sadat and Begin signed the peace accords between Egypt and Israel at Camp David under the sponsorship of the American president, Jimmy Carter. The final event of the Epilogue describes the birth of Dickstein's and Suza's son, whom they agree to call Towfik. These events balance the promise of the Prologue. Dickstein has the place of his own that he wanted, and he is at home with his family on the kibbutz. The reader has the satisfying sense that the story is complete and that the novel has been all that the narrator suggested it would be in the beginning.

The only detail after the Epilogue is a copy of a notice from the *London Daily Telegraph* in 1977, which quotes a dispatch from New York to the effect that Israel was suspected of hijacking some uranium nine years earlier. The inclusion of the actual news report locates *Triple* right in the middle of historical facts in just the way that Follett likes to suggest that his fiction plays with truth but only within intriguingly close proximity to it. The news clipping at the end thrusts the reader back simultaneously into the world of history and the world of the novel. This overlap between the excitement of historical events and the excitement of a fictional plot gives Follett's novels their most engaging aspect.

THEMATIC ISSUES

The novel's most persistent themes are the concern for the reconciliation of nationalism with ethnic and racial identity and the need for world peace in an age that threatens to use atomic weapons. In this sense the plot and the themes of the novel are direct reflections of each other in that the situation that drives the plot also articulates the major themes. Of course, any book dealing with war is also concerned about peace. But *Triple* focuses on the importance of obtaining peace by making war and war's effects on each character and relationship in the book. The inclusion of short, interpolated scenes about the Egyptian president talking to his wife about the need for peace and the characters' series of encounters with war keep the reader's attention on war, which thus becomes more than a plot device for an adventure story; it functions as a thematic concern for the book.

The novel also focuses on people's tendency to stereotype others who are in some ways different from them. The earliest cross-cultural misperceptions occur when Dickstein and Cortone are approaching Professor Ashford's house after Dickstein has told his friend that Ashford is interested in Semitic languages and culture and has married a Palestinian woman. Cortone is surprised that the house is in the Tudor style because he had expected something Moorish. The illogic behind his expectation is a minor example of the difficulty of creating and maintaining tolerance in the world. Similarly, Rostov is suspicious and contemptuous of his Arab allies, and Hassan is quick to use national and ethnic stereotypes to advance his plans. On the whole, Dickstein is relatively free from such cross-cultural suspicions, and his marriage to Suza as well as his campaign to have his children declared Israeli citizens suggest hope for a future where such cross-cultural connections can be positive and helpful.

Another reflection on the conflicts among nations arises also from Cortone, whose Mafia connections and lifestyle suggest an earlier version of how society might organize itself. The Mafia is essentially a form of social ordering predicated on a warrior mentality. The Mafia exists by preying on other people and keeping order and safety through direct threat and punishment. If nations want to keep order through higher principles than fear, especially when the threat comes from atomic weapons, then they need to find a better way to negotiate differences than the readily available, but deplorable, methods of the Mafia.

Cortone's presence in the novel offers another perspective on the theme of modern societies and their ways of establishing order: Cortone is the one who, however ineffectively, rises to the call of honor and gratitude. He alone is the one who acts solely because it is the honorable thing to do. He personally escorts Suza to Italy because he owes Dickstein his life and he sees taking steps to protect him as his duty. The effort costs him his life because he is so out of shape and alienated from the actual demands of a code of honor, and his gesture is seen in that ironic context. But Cortone's direct affirmation of honor and personal gratitude is a positive contrast to the mixed and petty motives of so many of the other characters in the novel. Rostov plays bureaucratic games, and the man from Euratom is vulnerable to Dickstein's blackmail because he is a cog in a large engine and to preserve his own place in the system he is willing to sacrifice the values of the system itself. Cortone may be ridiculous in his efforts to pay back his debt of honor, but he at least reminds the reader of a time when people saw a close connection between how they viewed the world and how they acted in it. The novel is careful to keep these perspectives in an ironic framework so that its reflections do not get too preachy. The fact that Cortone is noble and amiable in wartime activity and in pursuing personal business but is otherwise engaged in gangster-related activity asks the reader to think about these qualities but also to keep in mind that life in the twentieth century is complex.

LITERARY DEVICES

Triple continues Follett's characteristic careful and precise writing. His style keeps the action moving, as is appropriate for a thriller, but he is always careful to write with an eye for the complex figure of speech embedded in the narration. Suza's response to Hassan's sexual advances takes the form of a statement about the status of Arab women that beats the ideologue at his own game and then tells him that Arab men "need to learn the difference between being manly and being porcine"(258); the play on "porcine" refers both to the current use of "pig" as a term of contempt for men who have no respect for women and to the status of pork among Muslims as an unclean food.

Follett uses metaphors and similes often and carefully, usually with a dual purpose. For instance, the narrator compares Dickstein's feelings on seeing the *Coparelli* to feelings of lust for a woman, and then he mentions Suza: "When he saw her sweep slowly in, and read the name *Coparelli* on her side, and thought of the drums of yellowcake that would soon fill her belly, he was overcome by a most peculiar feeling, like the one he had when he looked at Suza's naked body . . . yes, almost like lust" (251). The simile draws upon a traditional habit of referring to ships as women. The narrator takes the comparison a little further when he specifies Dickstein's feelings about Suza. This specificity suggests to the reader how overwhelming his love for Suza is because she is always on his mind. Finally, the figure equates Dickstein's work in his spy mission with sex and so encourages the reader to see the kind of transference from sex to power that is characteristic in psychoanalytical analyses of political events. The simile operates, then, as a reminder of the political dimension of the novel, of the character development of Dickstein, and of the woman-centered dimensions of the novel.

The novel uses a metaphor in an extended and careful way when it presents Rostov's intense commitment to the pursuit of Dickstein. A paragraph that begins with a straightforward comparison of Rostov's state when engaged in a chess game with his approach to going after Dickstein ends with a metaphorical comparison of Rostov to a persistent animal tracker. This comparison emphasizes the bloodlust in the tracker and so suggests a predator rather than a tracking animal such as a bloodhound: "David Rostov's blood was up. He felt the way he did in a chess game when three or four of the opponent's moves began to form a pattern and he could see from where the attack would come and how he would have to turn it to a rout. . . . What moved him now, what kept him tense and alert and sharpened at the edge of his ruthlessness, was the thrill of the chase and the scent of the quarry in his nostrils" (136). The metaphor makes the equation between Rostov and a predator without making the comparison explicit. It reminds the reader that Rostov's pursuit is, paradoxically, both coldly logical, as in chess, and passionate and driven, as with a predator on the track of a wounded prey. The fact that the paragraph also includes Rostov's boss, Yuri Andropov, as one of his intended victims suggests the complexity of the chase for Rostov. In capturing Dickstein and foiling that plot, he will gain the upper hand in his internal struggle with Andropov for influence and power within the KGB. The metaphor enables Follett to emphasize to the reader the intensity and consequence of the chase.

The narrator's tone of voice calls attention to itself in a few places and reminds the reader that the narrator has a perspective as well. Early in the novel the narrator condescends toward one of the minor characters, a woman whom Dickstein follows from the Euratom building in Luxembourg to her home: "She parked in the cobbled yard of a square Luxembourgeois house with a nail-studded door" (55). The narrator uses the proper form for making a French noun into an adjective, but the word indicates superficial and poor taste in decorations and other matters of material values in the view of the narrator. The narrator reveals another personal perspective at the beginning of Chapter 10 when making a joke about Dickstein's establishment of the shell shipping corporation to hide his planned hijacking of the ship: "Nat Dickstein went to New York to become a shipping tycoon. It took him all morning" (188). The little joke based upon the ambiguities of what Dickstein is doing in comparison to what becoming a shipping tycoon would ordinarily take, reveals the narrator's comfort with Dickstein and his actions, a comfort that encourages the reader to sympathize with Dickstein. The narrator is never clearly and openly on Dickstein's side, but the warm and easy attitude that pervades the writing about him tells the reader that the narrator is certainly comfortable with Dickstein, and so the balance of the attitudes in the novel clearly lies with him.

A NEW HISTORICIST APPROACH TO *TRIPLE*

In considering the value and importance of literary works, literary critics have often taken into account the connections between the works and the times in which they were written. The critic looks beyond the literature to consider how the history that surrounds the work can help to explain its structure and strategy. What supports these investigations into the historical aspects of literary works is a conviction that the works themselves are innately valuable, so more information about the historical context will certainly add to an understanding of the text. But the critic regards the literary work as the embodiment of universal values and truths, independent of its historical context.

In recent decades some critics have taken the position that literary works are not necessarily embodiments of universals and so cannot be studied apart from their historical settings. These critics, called New Historicists, examine how the literary text is grounded in and shaped by its immediate social, political, and cultural contexts. This emphasis on contextual influence reduces the traditional belief that individual creativity is the sole source of literary art. The New Historicist examines the linguistic, social, political, and cultural traditions that influence literature and other works of art of a particular period. At times, such critics seem to approach literary works in the way that archaeologists approach ancient ruins: They attribute equal importance to every aspect and resist developing statements of meaning based upon one set of criteria to the exclusion of others. Indeed, one of the important influences on New Historicism, Michel Foucault, titled an early book *The Archaeology of Knowledge* (1969).

New Historicists are also interested in how responses to literary works change over time. They see the interaction of a work with its audience as central to its meaning. New Historicists are as interested in historical connections ignored by the texts as in those implicit in the texts. Consequently, they find themselves pursuing alternative readings of texts that enrich the reader's understanding.

Triple, like many Follett novels, seems at first glance to be explicitly grounded in history; it even ends with a Postscript consisting of a newspaper clipping reporting an event similar to the central premise of the novel. Indeed, the novel draws attention to its historical context. A New Historicist would focus not so much on the explicit historical context as on larger issues and concerns—about race, contested resources, and international political power—which are not examined in the novel. For instance, a New Historicist might ask that the novel pay closer attention to the deep and dividing differences in Middle Eastern politics before offering the marriage of Nat Dickstein and Suza Ashford as hope for long-lasting peace. The New Historicist might suggest that such a simplified line serves the international interests that want to resolve regional tensions at the expense of the religious and cultural traditions of indigenous peoples.

Triple makes only passing reference to the West's continuing dependence on the Middle East for oil and the rise of Islamic fundamentalism, two very important forces in shaping the events and the policies that dominated the Middle East in the late 1970s. Thinking about these two enormous historical forces highlights the restrictions the novel has imposed on its story. Traditional literary critics give novelists the option to include or exclude social and historical context as artistic design dictates, but New Historicists want to know why the writer omits the treatment of these pressing issues in a novel about a particular area. The New Historicist might emphasize the desperation of actions such as the Israeli hijacking and the Arab and Soviet counter moves in a world where both businesses and governments can obviate the effects of heroic deeds by agreements to give or withhold arms. While the conventions of spy thrillers encourage readers to celebrate the novel's actions, the historical context reminds us that such valor and dedication on that level may be undercut when set against the backdrop of the Middle East in 1968, the setting of the novel, or in 1979, the year of publication.

New Historicists suggest also that readers develop a historical consciousness about the connections between a literary work and the reader's own historical context. Whatever the connections *Triple* has with 1968 or 1979, a reader must recognize that forces and values of his own historical period shape his or her engagement with the book. The reader's own perspective, shaped by social, political, and cultural considerations, is a necessary part of the interpretive process and enriches the reading of the work.

6

The Key to Rebecca
(1980)

Perhaps the key to *The Key to Rebecca* is *Rebecca*, Daphne DuMaurier's 1938 novel about English aristocratic traditions. Ken Follett establishes parallels with and differences from *Rebecca* and uses both to advance his plot, establish his characters, and introduce thematic concerns. The plot connections are slight, since Follett could have used any novel published in the late 1930s to act as the source of the coded messages the spy sends to his handlers in Berlin; but the choice of *Rebecca* invites comparisons. The parallels with characters are more important. The nameless heroine of *Rebecca* is a stranger to Manderley, the English country house that is the setting for the novel, and she finds it difficult to fit in with the cultured and elegant ways of the house even after she is its mistress. Similarly, Elene Fontana, the heroine of *The Key to Rebecca*, has to work to imagine that she could be accepted as a lover by William Vandam, the novel's hero, or as an equal by his world. Just as the heroine of *Rebecca* has to come to terms with the ghostly presence of Rebecca, the deceased first wife of Mr. DeWinters, the master of the house, Elene must contend with the memory of Vandam's deceased wife, Angela, a cool, elegant, and controlling aristocrat. These parallels remind the reader of the extraordinary barriers that lie between Elene and William Vandam. The pervasive presence of the English country house and its wealth of aristocratic traditions in *Rebecca* is in stark contrast to the open spaces and Bedouin culture of Egypt and the nouveau riche aspects of the British forces. Furthermore, the actual wealth that sustains English country houses has been amassed in part through the development and maintenance of the British Empire, and so the house is a reminder of how Britain came to be in control of Egypt. Aristocratic elegance occurs simultaneously with the iron will that dominated the conquered peoples, leading to the secret work of Kemel and other Egyptian soldiers to free Egypt from British rule, which becomes part of *The Key to Rebecca*'s plot.

As a thriller, *The Key to Rebecca* combines a number of the features of Follett's previous two thrillers, *Eye of the Needle* and *Triple*. Like *Eye*, the novel is set during World War II and centers on British efforts to catch a master German spy in order to have a chance at winning the war. This spy also carries a knife and uses it with great skill, and the goal, defeating Rommel in the African desert, is one that is already well known to the reader as an important event in World War II, just as *Eye* revolved around discovering the plans for the D-Day invasion. Like *Triple*, the novel is set in the Middle East and invests a lot of time and energy in the details of Middle Eastern culture. *The Key to Rebecca* also involves a heroine who is of a different race and culture from those of the hero and so brings to the fore issues of cross-cultural tolerance and racial bias. In *Key* the problem of cross-cultural interaction is complicated by the fact that the heroine is Jewish, posing as an Arab, and the spy is Germanborn but raised as an Arab.

POINT OF VIEW

The point of view in *The Key to Rebecca* follows the pattern set in most Follett novels: the story is told from the point of view of an all-knowing narrator who sees into the minds of the characters. The narration shifts from one main character to another, giving the reader a sense of the important influences and decisions that drive the action. This narrative strategy combines the vast perspective of the all-knowing narrator with the intimate knowledge allowed through a point of view that centers in the consciousness of a character.

The novel opens with a tightly focused narrative point of view. The reader is introduced to one of the main characters engaged in a heroic struggle to complete a journey on foot across the desert. The opening sentence—"The last camel collapsed at noon" (3)—thrusts the reader right into the middle of the action and creates the sense of crisis that is essential to giving a sense of its importance. The significance of camels to someone in a desert and the fact that the desert is the most dangerous at noon heighten the reader's recognition that he or she must pay attention to what happens next. This close focus on the character in the desert remains even after he finds some nomads in the desert who are his cousins. In the interactions with these Bedouins the point of view remains that of the all-knowing narrator, but the narrator reveals all of what Achmed, the desert traveler, is thinking and very little about what the others around him are thinking. The narrator relates the memories that Achmed has, memories that fill in some of the background on how he comes to be traversing the desert. The point of view stays consistent throughout the chapter as the desert wanderer, Achmed, transforms himself into Alexander Wolff, a German spy headed for Cairo under the pretext of being a European businessman. The point of view brings the reader quickly into the action of the story and the fortunes of one of the chief characters.

In the early chapters especially, the narrative makes a point of overlapping the action so that the end of one chapter becomes the opening of the next chapter but as experienced by another character. At the end of Chapter 2 one of the major characters, Vandam, is searching the house of a murder suspect to find out something about his identity. Chapter 3 opens with the suspected murderer, Alexander Wolff, crouching outside the house waiting for Vandam to leave. Wolff's anger and frustration at being forced to hide outside his own house is a preview of the feelings he has about his mission, and his interest in the identity of the soldier searching the house anticipates the rivalry that will deepen between the two men as the novel proceeds. The overlapping point of view increases the intensity of the focus and enables Follett to develop some emphases that will become important to the novel's thematic and narrative progress.

Most of the novel is told through the experiences and activities of the characters. Each of the early chapters is told from the point of view of one character, although some chapters include a second character's point of view. In one instance, the all-knowing narrator tells the reader what is going on in the German camps where the spy will send his messages. As the action gets more complex and the suspense grows, the chapters include more than one point of view on the action. The increasingly abrupt shifts as the action heats up add to the mounting tension.

The novel uses the first-person point of view in two places, a shift in perspective that is unusual when so much of the rest of the novel is told by an omniscient narrator. In the first instance, the novel introduces the thoughts of the twelve-year-old Anwar el-Sadat at the beginning of a chapter where he appears as a minor character, although, as the reader knows, Sadat is headed for a major role in Egyptian history. The thoughts of the child are presented without any introduction. They are followed by the reappearance of the all-knowing point of view describing the activities and thoughts of Sadat at twenty-two, but the inset is not presented as a memory. Rather, it is a glance at the background that drives much of the action of the novel and offers a rare perspective on the British presence in Egypt and the origins of Egyptian nationalism. The second use of the first-person point of view occurs later in the novel as the chase grows hectic and the conflict becomes more of a one-on-one fight. At the beginning of chapter 26 the direct first-person point of view of Wolff, then Vandam, and then Elene adds to the sense of crisis and the suspense that the novel needs to maintain its pace and make good on its promise as a thriller.

CHARACTER DEVELOPMENT

The Key to Rebecca introduces its readers to Alexander Wolff, master spy and chief enemy to British counterespionage, as a heroic figure capable of overcoming extraordinary hardships in order to achieve his mission. The crossing of the desert, which so many of the locals find hard to imagine, is a measure of the lengths Wolff will go to obtain what he wants. Throughout the novel he shows resourcefulness, courage, determination, and extraordinary intelligence in gaining his objectives and eluding his pursuers. Wolff seems to be at home both in the desert and in sophisticated city settings, and he regards himself as capable of being a master of the whole world. His conversations reveal his enthusiasm for Nazi successes and the prospect of a world under German domination. At points in the novel his thoughts reveal that this deep commitment to Nazism might arise from some childhood traumas having to do with the death of his father and the sudden adjustment to a stepfather and to a new culture and a new home. Wolff talks to his cousin about the greatness of the Nazi regime and tells Elene that in a world that he sees as divided into masters and slaves he sees himself as one of the masters.

Wolff represents many of the paradoxical elements in the mix of cultures in the Middle East at the time of World War II. He is German but was raised as an Arab. He is dedicated to Germany as if it were his hand with him. She exercises such great power in private and in her public performances because she is in close touch with the deep psychosexual drives that animate her dancing and her private life. She draws on the deep conflicts and neuroses that haunt her inner life to shape her extraordinary dancing. The reader sees Sonja as a person driven to cruel and barbaric treatment of other people because of what she feels is the savage treatment she has received throughout her life. Sonja is introduced as a sensualist and a self-centered person. Her willingness to exploit both friends and enemies alienates her from the reader even as the reader is likely to find her fascinating and the sections of the novel involving her interesting and provocative. When Vandam uses personal humiliation to break her at the end, the reader is prepared to accept her debasement because Vandam needs the information to save people that the reader values and because Sonja has put herself outside the values that would warrant compassion for her. The demons that have plagued her life have perhaps turned her into a monster, and her capture at the end means not much more than the end of that monster.

PLOT DEVELOPMENT

Like many spy thrillers, *The Key to Rebecca* begins with a spy making an incursion into enemy territory in search of something badly needed by the spy's side, in this case information about the attack and defense plans of the British tank corps engaged at that time in a series of battles with the German general Erwin Rommel. Follett introduces a twist in this spy story from the outset in that Wolff comes into enemy territory that is actually his home and a place with which he is very familiar, and this familiarity makes him all the more dangerous and harder to capture. A spy's best weapon on such an incursion is to remain undetected, but that weapon is denied to Wolff almost from the beginning when his presence is detected by Vandam, once Vandam reads the report of the murder of the sergeant Wolff killed in Assyut. With a few phone calls Vandam identifies Wolff and so is on the spy's trail from the very beginning of the action.

The straightforward story of a spy being chased by a spy hunter remains the central plot of the novel. The chase takes on the character of a cat-and-mouse game confined to the city of Cairo, although the last few chapters resolve the action into a linear chase from Cairo to the south and into the desert. The series of traps and close calls for both opponents

homeland, but his only home is in Cairo. He is dispossessed of that home by the British as soon as they suspect him of murder, and so even his second home has been usurped by the British presence in Egypt. The alienation that he feels as he wanders the streets trying to find a place to light echoes the multiple conflicts that swirl through Middle Eastern politics at the time. The war in Europe might have a clear and definite set of oppositions, but the conflicts in Egypt are much more complex.

At the beginning of the novel, Wolff is the person in control, with the character to achieve his goals. He regularly gets the best of Vandam, his chief opponent, and on two occasions he delivers information to the German forces that enables them to defeat the British in important battles and to threaten Cairo itself. Toward the end of the novel the Germans are almost to Cairo and the British are making preparations to abandon the city and perhaps their presence in Africa, achievements directly attributable to Wolff. But Wolff soon is forced into the role of the pursued. In the opening chapter he gives a British soldier his correct name. This slight error makes it possible for Vandam to identify him and begin the process of pursuit early in the novel. At the end of chapter 1, another slip forces Wolff to kill a British soldier, a swift and deadly act that impresses the reader with his resolve and skill but leads to further pursuit and eventually capture. His control, which he needs in order both to carry out his mission and maintain his view of himself as a master of the world, erodes as the novel proceeds. His gradual decline into a driven madman making war on children corroborates the reader's sense of him as despicable and perhaps evil. The introduction of Wolff as heroic sharply contrasts with his miserable end in a cramped cell, the fate he feared the most.

The novel introduces Vandam, Wolff's opponent and the novel's hero, in a quite unheroic fashion. The reader first encounters Vandam as he wakes up after a night of too much gin and too many cigarettes, suffering muscle pain and soreness from playing cricket while being out of shape. Vandam's chief complaints seem to be the oppressive Egyptian heat and the tedium of his life, traits that are in stark contrast to Wolff's extraordinary physical stamina and achievements as well as the clear sense of purpose and determination with which he is introduced in the previous chapter. Vandam is different from other heroes in thrillers in that he is a career army man, not the amateur-called-to-duty that Follett and other authors have used so effectively. Vandam's job is intelligence, and he is doing a bad job of it, although his reaction to the news about the soldier Wolff killed shows him to be alert and perceptive. Certainly, Vandam is a cut above his commanding officer, Lieutenant Colonel Reggie Bogge, a petty and jealous army bureaucrat who seeks glory by thwarting any attempts of his staff to do something outstanding or by stealing the credit when they do. The novel is clear about Vandam's impatience with Bogge, and readers welcome Vandam's willingness to ignore or sidestep Bogge's authority to follow what the reader knows is important information. Bogge seems to stand for all that can go wrong in the army of a fading empire, while Vandam stands as the remnant of the spirit that made the nation great in the first place. He articulates this quality as "decency" in his thinking about what makes the British different from the Germans as occupiers of Egypt. His behavior throughout the novel convinces the reader that he is in fact decent and that decency counts for something, even if it no longer seems to be the same quality that built the British Empire.

Vandam changes throughout the novel in inverse relation to Wolff. As Wolff gradually declines, Vandam improves. He focuses on the chase and connects with other people, particularly Elene Fontana. Vandam's efforts throughout much of the novel lead to one dead end after another; indeed, the novel might not be able to include even one more failed trap for Wolff without becoming humorous. Only Vandam's steady intelligence and unflappable persistence enables him to keep after Wolff and finally defeat him, although he needs the help of Elene and his son, Billy, to overcome Wolff finally. In a conversation with Elene after they have made love, Vandam responds to her accusation that he does not care about people by telling her that she is having the same trouble that others have had with his "equanimity," and he explains to her its advantages for him and for those around him. She counters that he should show people his feelings. He seems willing to try. The reader notices that Vandam does try to change his ways and is thus more sympathetic as a character. His decision to delay rescuing his beloved and his son until Wolff can lead him to what Vandam needs to complete his intelligence mission is made with "equanimity." The stiff upper lip that is often associated with British character is here put into a favorable light and becomes almost a synonym for reason and justice. Vandam makes the tough decision to leave Elene and Billy in Wolff's hands for extra time because he can see the long-term consequences that argue for such restraint. By the end of the novel, he embodies and is surrounded by the values and the qualities that endear him to the reader. He becomes a hero not by his single and extraordinary actions but by his dedication to the small set of values and commitments that he knows to be true. Van-

dam's success in the novel gives the reader a sense of completeness because the hero gathers up within himself the set of virtues that the reader needs to see in place to feel that the action of the novel can safely come to a rest.

The novel introduces Elene in a series of negative definitions: she is unhappy that yet another lover has cast her off, she is living a false identity as an Arab woman when she is, in fact, Jewish, and she has no basis for regarding her choices as better for her than other alternatives. The reflections (and they are literally reflections since she develops her thinking as she looks at herself in the mirror) that reveal these crises of identity push her to apply at the Jewish Agency for permission to emigrate to Palestine. That spontaneous decision leads to her introduction to Vandam and her involvement in the action of the novel. Elene is a person without the convictions and commitments that define other characters, but her sense of herself and her basic values make her credible as the heroine who will step into the role needed to complete the action of the novel. The novel treats Elene's decision to make a clean start without pretenses in Palestine as ironic since the first thing Vandam asks her to do is to pose as a shopkeeper's assistant. Once she makes contact with Wolff, and for the rest of the novel, she is forced into one deception after another until by the end she is good enough at deception to create pretenses and fool Wolff. She is so good at her role that she delays Wolff's plans to send out his most important secret, a delay that proves to be his undoing. Elene's lack of certainty about her identity makes it doubly hard for her to think of herself as taking the place of Vandam's first wife. In a sense she earns her credentials and her place by making the complete and immediate commitment to ensure that Vandam's son, Billy survives his capture by Wolff. By the end of the novel, Elene has create the positive place for herself in the world which she so thoroughl lacked.

Sonja el-Aram is introduced as a person who has it all yet is vulnerab to the pressure that Wolff applies to induce her to take him in and the help him in his mission. She helps Wolff because she hates the Briti and because Wolff can keep her supplied with the sensual delights from food to sex—that she craves. As the most popular belly dancer Cairo, Sonja wields considerable power. When Vandam arrests her t first time, she gets the upper hand in the interrogation and leaves h without any of the information he had hoped to gain. She is very se sitive to issues of power and independence and pressures Wolff to ma her requests top priority as soon as she senses that she has the up]

creates the tension in the novel and raises the reader's expectations from chapter to chapter as Wolff grows bolder and more desperate and Vandam becomes more frustrated at Wolff's success in eluding him and as the stakes for catching him rise higher and higher. The overlapping points of view used in a number of chapters work to increase pace by creating a sense of proximity and familiarity between the two men. The novel complicates their duel of wits and nerves by revealing clues to the fact that Wolff has been the spy who rescued another important Arab spy and killed a woman working for the British in the process; failure to catch him was the only major flop in Vandam's intelligence career. The chase is complicated as well by the fact that each of the opponents uses a woman to disguise his actions and to set traps for information (Wolff) and for spies (Vandam).

The action to catch the spy and to elude the pursuer is set against the evolving romance between Elene and Vandam and the somewhat parallel, mutually self-serving relationship between Sonja and Wolff. When the novel introduces Vandam as a widower whom many people see in need of a wife and then Elene as a woman who has been rejected in love too often, the attraction between them seems inevitable in spite of their differences. By contrast Wolff's and Sonja's union arises out of need, fear, and lust and operates as a balance of power. Sonja articulates this lack of feeling: "It must be unusual, she thought, for two people to be so close and yet love each other so little" (89). The dynamics of the male-female relationships affect Wolff's ability to operate and Vandam's to chase him. The plot at times moves forward as much by emotional response, for example, to a tone of voice, as to the onward pressure of plans and outside events.

The actions of the Egyptian nationalists play a minor but important part in the development of the plot. The complications that the nationalists introduce both help and hinder Wolff. He has contempt for their aspirations and their plans, but he needs their cooperation to keep his operation secret and viable. The ill-fated flight of the Egyptian nationalists to reach Rommel is both tragic and comic. Their justifiable and deep convictions about being rid of British rule are laudable, but their naiveté in pursuing these aspirations leads to a foolish flight and a bungled attempt to pressure Wolff into helping them.

The action of *The Key to Rebecca* is organized around the three major tank battles of the 1942 campaign in Africa: Tobruk, Mersa Matruh, and Alam Halfa. The novel suggests that the first two British defeats were the result of Wolff's intelligence reports, and those sections end with the announcements that Tobruk and Mersa Matruh have fallen. Not until Vandam puts his brilliant counterintelligence plan into action do the British succeed in crushing Rommel. The structure of the novel keeps the focus on the spy story: the novel begins with the spy crossing the desert to enter Cairo and ends with the spy in a cell and the hero out in the desert enjoying a picnic in the middle of a seemingly miraculous appearance of desert flowers after a sudden rain.

THEMATIC ISSUES

One of the novel's major thematic concerns is the need for a positive and productive sense of self. This need surfaces early in Wolff's many disguises, which reflect his confused sense of self and his need to pursue actions that portray him as the master of the world he longs to dominate. These convictions about his own grandeur continue despite the fact that he spends most of his time skulking around Cairo, on more than one occasion hiding in water or mud. Vandam's identity problem, Elene tells him, is that he does not have an identity; that is, because he has allowed people access only to his public persona, he avoids true personal relationships. Elene has this same concern when she wonders who she is and where she belongs (46). The novel brings each of the characters to some realization about identity: Elene finds a home and a role with Vandam; Vandam finds that he can open up and be committed to another person; and Wolff is at last forced to face, literally, the cramped dimensions of his destiny.

National identity drives much of the novel's action. The British and the Germans have alternating respect and contempt for each other. Both despise, often for racist reasons, the Arab citizens that they are fighting to rule. The novel depends upon the reader's sense of right and wrong to keep up the interest in a spy novel, which has to have protagonists and antagonists. But the characters in the novel are not wholly good or evil. The Germans are evil in some respects, but they are also soldiers trying to do their best under the pressure of dealing with stupid and venal hierarchies. The British have race and class prejudices that make the reader skeptical of casting them in the role of heroes. Vandam's speculations on probable reactions to his falling in love with Elene make many of these attitudes clear: "It was, of course, a disaster that he and Elene had fallen so joyfully in love. His parents, his friends and the Army would be aghast at the idea of his marrying a wog. His mother would also feel bound to explain why the Jews were wrong to reject Jesus" (227). The Anglo-Egyptian Union, "a club for bored Europeans" (25), exists to pretend that there is some commerce between the rulers and the ruled, but it is actually an example of racist social structures. The novel regularly complicates the portrayals of nationalities enough to make the question, What does it mean to be British? or German? or Arab? or Jewish? a sustained focus of the book. Wolff offers his view about slaves and masters. As Vandam watches his fellow officers accept defeat so easily, he thinks about the Battle of Britain and the mix of virtues that has characterized the British people.

Although *The Key to Rebecca* recognizes the importance of opposing evil and defending traditions and values, it suggests that wars of national interests may be fruitless, even for the victors, and that a lasting peace lies in transcending national loyalties. The battles won and lost are important, but their significance and consequences are often at odds with the aims of the opponents. Rommel would have defeated the British long before the opening of the novel had he been supplied adequately. The British in their turn might or might not have won their battles if the spy had not been successful, but the narrow margin that makes the huge difference suggests that wars among nations defy the categories that comprise the rhetoric of nationalism and the elements of jingoistic novels. The happy resolution that Vandam and Elene find suggests that nationalistic traditions should give way to a sense of pursuing an identity and that this common human project should help peoples to live and thrive together in the world. The twists in world politics changed the lives of Sonja and Wolff for the worse and left them twisted individuals capable of bringing only harm into the world. Presumably, positive work among nations may create healthy people and enable them to lead productive lives.

LITERARY DEVICES

The DuMaurier novel *Rebecca* is alluded to not only in Follett's title but often in the text. The use of literary allusions continues when Billy Vandam, talking with Elene about the detective novels they both read, suggests that she read some Raymond Chandler and she recommends Georges Simenon. Follett's novel makes a series of references to "tec" novels as mere entertainments, thus casting a self-reflective look at a closely related genre (211). The allusion to Agatha Christie's novel *Death on the Nile* is at first glance a casual detail, but since it comes at a moment when things look bad for the British forces, the unintended threat suggested by the title applies also to Vandam and the other British soldiers (133). The novel alludes as well to Charles Dickens's *Oliver Twist* when a policeman explains who Abdullah is by comparing him to Fagin, the master of young thieves and pickpockets (67).

The language in *The Key to Rebecca* is not especially self-conscious, but the narrator regularly uses similes. Wolff, wandering about the city looking for a place to stay, is described as feeling like "a rat in a maze" (33), and the Egyptian plane crashing after being hit by German fire is said to hit the desert and burst into flames "like a blossom opening its petals" (77). Wolff darting in front of Vandam's headlight in the alley behind the restaurant is compared to "a knife slicing the flame" (158) just a few sentences before Wolff uses his knife on Vandam.

Some details in the novel are revelatory beyond their function as details. Sonja's houseboat, for instance, suggests her lack of roots or solid connections with her world. Vandam's motorcycle suggests his individualistic stance and his loneliness as well as the streak of restlessness and abandon that appears occasionally in his personality. When Bogge insists that Vandam pay more attention to organizing another cricket match than to catching Wolff, the British passion for their national sport at the expense of the unit's wartime mission becomes a measure of the softness of the British Army. The taxi that Wolff rents for his picnic with Elene is large and plush, suggesting his imperial sense of himself. Vandam's servant, Gaafar, behaves like an English butler; this little affectation reveals character when Vandam mentions to someone that Gaafar will take good care of someone as long as the person does not treat him like a "wog." Gaafar's behavior makes an important distinction between serving someone and being treated like a servant, a distinction that emphasizes one of the book's main thematic concerns.

A PSYCHOANALYTICAL APPROACH TO *THE KEY TO REBECCA*

A psychoanalytical approach to reading literature offers insight into character motivation. Sigmund Freud, the founder of psychoanalysis in the late nineteenth century, suggested that the human psyche is made up of three parts: the id, the unconscious part of the psyche where forbidden desires and urges exist; the ego, the conscious part of the psyche that operates in an orderly and reasonable fashion and is usually regarded as the self; and the superego, the ethical conscience of the self. Freud suggested that these parts of a person's psyche were often in strife, with the id uninhibitedly seeking pleasure and the ego and superego resisting, more or less, those urges. Freud suggested that the push and pull of the conscious and the unconscious mind was normal and that adult behavior is determined by the way a person negotiated these competing urges while growing up. Freud carefully examined childhood and adolescence, beginning with an infant's connections with its mother and father.

Freud suggested that an infant first experiences the world as it nurses at its mother's breast and this experience of comfort and pleasure is mixed with early sexual feelings; therefore, a child begins its life with complex feelings of both affection and desire for its mother, none of which is any real problem until the child loses those comforts and pleasures as it is weaned. At about that time the child begins to perceive the father as the one who also receives pleasure and comfort from the mother, so a child, especially a boy, may develop a sense of rivalry with the father for the mother. Freud called this stage in personality development the "Oedipus complex," after the Greek tragic hero Oedipus, who unwittingly, but not without contributing reasons, kills his father and marries his mother. This rivalry of the son and father for the mother's affections can become problematic if the child experiences some major injury or loss and blames the father. The rivalry sometimes extends to the child's fears that the father will castrate him to deprive him completely of the mother's presence. As the child grows, the explicit and conscious fears and desires are pushed into the unconscious, but they still operate by prompting actions driven by desire or fear but appearing to the person to be arising from some other, more respectable motive. These tendencies of the mind to cloak repressed unconscious desires in the appearances of virtuous and publicly acceptable actions are called displacements; they make it difficult for people to understand some of the motives for their actions.

A psychoanalytical reading of *The Key to Rebecca* invites recognition of the importance of the psychological aspects of personality. The novel takes great pains to include a lot of material on childhood experiences and then suggests that they are the source of at least some of the characters' adult behavior. Sonja's insistence on playing out an infantile sexual fantasy in the lovemaking that Wolff arranges for her with Elene and himself is perhaps the most explicit representation of psychoanalytical theory in the novel. Sonja insists that lovemaking recreates the childhood pattern of rejection that she experienced as she watched her father and mother making love and tried to compete with her mother for her father's attentions. This unconscious libidinal desire for a father and competition with a mother is called the Electra complex after another character in a Greek play and is parallel to the Oedipus complex. Sonja appears to feel she is fulfilled sexually and emotionally only when she can recreate this childhood trauma with a ménage à trois and then enact a symbolic victory for herself over her mother by finally having intercourse with the man in the trio and denying such success to the other woman. Follett makes it clear that Sonja is defined by her neuroses. She hates the British because they killed her father, the person who still dominates her emotional life. Wolff controls Sonja by acting like a father-figure to her, bringing her treats and providing her with the sexual fulfillment she cannot have without the fantasy element of seducing her father.

The novel suggests that Wolff also is driven by his childhood traumas. He talks about how he has been deprived of a father twice—once by death and a second time by political exile—and imagines himself compensated for his losses by fulfilling a role of master in the new order he expects the victorious Germans to establish, thus becoming the powerful figure he feels he lost by his father's death. Wolff's development in the novel is presented as a regression back to childhood, ending with him curled in an almost fetal position in the cramped space of his cell. At the beginning of the novel he is in control and takes the role of the master in approaching his various tasks, including manipulating people to his own ends; he is a person acting out of conscious and reasonable motives. As he meets with obstacles and opposition, he makes his conflicts more and more personal and becomes less and less in control of himself. By the end of the novel, his rivalry with Vandam reduces his effectiveness, and his mistakes in judgment lead to his capture and imprisonment. This regression offers a psychological explanation for his career as a spy and for his final downfall.

The novel focuses on Vandam's distanced relationship with women and then suggests that it was shaped by a childhood encounter with sex and an angry parent. Vandam's connections with women are discussed by the narrator, the British community in Cairo, and Elene very soon after she meets him. Vandam himself does not think about it much. His wife is described as having been cool, elegant, and distant. At the end of Chapter 4 Vandam relaxes at a whorehouse that features hashish and young girls. In the grip of the hashish, he hallucinates about the identity of his prostitute and imagines various other women he knows in that role. This imaginary projection suggests a psychoanalytical dimension even if Vandam takes no note of it. The reader is alerted to the sexual and sensuous content of his action. The origin of his behavior is suggested at the end of chapter 8 when Vandam remembers his moment of sexual awakening at eleven years old on accidentally seeing his eight-year-old cousin step out of the bath. His mother slapped him and screamed, "Get out!" The event and the memory of it are shaping moments in Vandam's psychological past. From this point Vandam's relationship with Elene takes on a special undercurrent because the reader is watching to see if he will grow out of this childhood pattern. In fact, he does, and the novel ends in a healthy adult relationship with Elene, a psychological change that offers the reader a different sort of victory.

Elene seems to be the most psychologically healthy person in the novel. She is clear in her own mind about the nature of her actions. She is a person who has, in fact, been rejected by her father, which she regrets, but she understands it and places it in the kind of context that avoids the neuroses of displaced psychological trauma. It is Elene who makes Vandam recognize his pretenses and his defenses, which enables him to mature in his approach to women. She analyzes his behavior accurately and her responses to his recognitions are mature and helpful.

The war itself can be seen from a psychoanalytical perspective as arising out of neurotic approaches to power and domination. The terms for making the equation between power and domination are introduced in the relationship of Wolff and Sonja. The desire of nations for conquest is articulated, often in the language of international politics, in terms similar to those used for sexual relations. The motives and behaviors of both the British and the Germans appear as a mixture of dark subconscious desires and altruistic and self-righteous purposes that compete with them. The site for negotiating these desires and purposes is the shadow world of Cairo, which has no clear identity and so is more open to the manifestation of illicit and otherwise repressed desires. Certainly Vandam's recreations are more outrageous than what was accepted among the British population. The greatest celebrity of the city is a belly dancer who wants to go to Berlin because it is the apex of decadence in her eyes. The streets of Cairo are inhabited by corrupt policemen and Abdullah's hordes. In this world of blurred boundaries, the distinctions between right and wrong are emphasized as they are harder to establish and maintain. The novel uses this indistinct ground to concentrate attention on motives and values by baring the psychological drives that motivate all the characters.

A psychoanalytical reading of the novel emphasizes the psychological forces influencing the decisions characters make, the courses nations pursue, and the development of cultures. Sensitivity to the importance of a healthy father-son relationship enables the reader to recognize the pathological dimension of Wolff's actions and discern a weakness in a character who at times seems invincible. Sonja's projection of her childhood traumas onto her adult sexual relationships leads to her downfall. The reader recognizes that Vandam has some worrisome psychological traits and so welcomes his entry into a healthy relationship with Elene. These aspects of psychological interest add to the drama and the tension of the novel and intensify the experience for the reader. Psychoanalytical approaches usually add to the meaning of a novel rather than compete with meanings generated by other approaches because the dynamic of psychoanalytical theory applies to most human situations.

7

The Man from St. Petersburg
(1982) and
Lie Down with Lions
(1986)

Both *The Man from St. Petersburg* and *Lie Down with Lions* are spy thrillers. Both concern a moment in history when the fortunes of an important event depend on the actions of the main characters. In short, both are like other Ken Follett novels written before and since. Those similarities, however, serve to emphasize the very different uses Follett makes of his fictional situations. The plot of each novel concludes with a chase, but one (*Man*) concludes within the confines of a single house while the other (*Lions*) ends with a chase up and down miles and miles of mountain ranges and across an international border. Both novels begin with a spy entering a hostile environment to achieve a specific mission, but in both books the roles of spy and hunter become reversed at least once. Follett follows through on his promise to provide thrilling spy stories, but he seems to regard the formula as a challenge on which to develop interesting variations. The experiments in these novels mark them as new and innovative entries into a familiar Follett territory even as they confirm his mastery of these recognizable literary types.

THE MAN FROM ST. PETERSBURG

Like other Follett novels, *The Man from St. Petersburg* takes place at a moment of historical importance, here the summer of 1914, just before the assassination of the Austrian Archduke Francis Ferdinand and the onset of World War I. Historians have regarded the beginning of that war as especially interesting because of the dense and complex factors that contributed to it. Thus, any focus on events at the center of the European political maelstrom in 1914 becomes itself a matter of narrative importance. Follett bases *The Man from St. Petersburg* on the premise that one of the crucial alliances at the beginning of World War I was the agreement of Russia to enter the anticipated war on Britain's side against Germany because to do so would force Germany to maintain an eastern and a western front, creating a strain on its already considerable military power. The British attempt to reach agreement with the Russians through the friendship between Stephen, Lord Walden, a very conservative British aristocrat, and his nephew by marriage, Prince Aleksey Andreyevich Orlov, a thirty-year-old Russian admiral and Czar Nicholas's deputy to deal with the British. The novel makes it clear that Walden dislikes the young Winston Churchill for political and social reasons when Churchill comes to Walden Hall to ask his host to undertake the negotiations. Walden accepts the charge when the king asks him to do it and when it becomes clear that he has a taste for this kind of diplomacy. His task is to entertain Orlov at his house and to negotiate with him the terms for the alliance.

The plot of the novel arises from the decision of a deeply committed Russian revolutionary to assassinate Orlov in London in order to undercut the negotiations and so save the Russian peasantry from being forced into a war that cannot serve their interests. The introduction of the revolutionary, Felix Kschessinsky, sets up the conflict that moves the action. The destruction of the power of the privileged classes is the explicit motive for Kschessinsky's revolutionary activities and is a theme throughout the novel. His dedication to working for an ideal form of government, or at least an end to those governments that oppress common people, has impelled him toward political action since his youth. This mission to kill Orlov and sabotage the secret treaty becomes the primary concern of the reader early in the novel.

The theme of power and class differences is introduced in the opening pages in Walden's aversion to meeting with Churchill. To Walden, Churchill represents all that is wrong with the current Liberal government in England and with the modern world in general. The divisions between the two men remind the reader that distinctions about class, money, and power shape many of the large and small decisions made by nations. The values and issues implicit in those historic events leading up to

World War I can still be felt on the stage of world politics today, even though the Hapsburg Empire is long gone.

Point of View

Like other Follett novels, *The Man from St. Petersburg* uses an omniscient narrator who keeps the reader informed about all the aspects of the unfolding story including the thoughts and memories of the characters. The directness of the action and the immediacy with which the reader is thrust into it require the narrator to convey important background information through lengthy and detailed memories that come flooding back to the central characters as their associations with events and people arise. In the first chapter the mention of her nephew, Aleks, brings to Lydia, Lady Walden, memories of another young Russian: "It was nineteen years since she had seen that man, but still the mere mention of St. Petersburg could bring him to mind and make her skin crawl beneath the watered silk of her gown" (11). So the reader gains an early insight into Lydia's deep secrets and senses the complex relationships that will make the negotiations with Orlov more than a straightforward political matter. Later in that chapter Kschessinsky's reason for coming to England is presented through a memory of a meeting he attended back in Russia: "And in Geneva he had made the decision which brought him to England. He recalled that meeting. He had almost missed it." (23)

The narrator tells most of the story from the specific points of view of the various central characters but sometimes fills in details and offers perspectives that individual characters do not have in order to help the reader understand the elements of plot or the significance of issues and values. Points of view of the individual characters advance or slow the action as needed. Most of the chapters shift among a number of perspectives; some primarily serve the interests of plot; others reveal more about a character's frame of mind, values, or development. This narrative strategy is similar to those of other Follett novels.

As in *The Key to Rebecca*, Follett uses overlapping points of view, but here he combines them with the novelistic equivalent of the movie cliffhanger. The end of chapter 3 is told from Kschessinsky's point of view as he stalks Orlov to Orlov's hotel room intent on getting the door open enough for him to throw in the nitroglycerin bomb he has made. As he opens the door, he discovers that Basil Thompson, the Scotland Yard detective, and Stephen Walden have set a trap for him. Retreating into the hall, he threatens them with his explosive liquid and then tosses the vial at them in an attempt to run away fast enough to avoid injury from the explosion. The chapter ends with the vial in midair. Chapter 4 opens with Stephen Walden's point of view as he dives to catch the nitroglycerin and prevent it from hitting the floor. The reader gets a breathtaking narrative sequence and the full sense and thrill of the danger by seeing the action from the perspectives of the persons most immediately involved. The manipulation of point of view in this instance serves the purposes of a spy thriller well.

Follett makes surprising use of point of view in the Epilogue when the narrator drops the usual impersonal pose and speaks directly to the reader. The final sentence offers a sentiment that could come only from someone with a personality and presence independent enough to think that the reader will be comforted by the expression of that sentiment. The Epilogue describes the career and life of Charlotte, the biological daughter of Lydia and Kschessinsky and the acknowledged daughter of Walden, after the fire at Walden Hall and the death of Kschessinsky. In her nineties, Charlotte reports that she is reading A. I. Solzhenitsyn's *The Gulag Archipelago* and thinks she will not finish it until she's ninety-nine. The narrator then adds, "Somehow I think she'll make it" (342). Follett seems to want the reader to fix on the positive sentiments surrounding this character as a way to end the novel.

Character Development

The "man" of the title and the person who creates most of the novel's action is Feliks Kschessinsky, the Russian revolutionary described at one point as feeling happy for the first time in years as he comes close to his attempt at assassination (44). Flashbacks reveal the events that brought him to such a state. In pre-Revolutionary Russia, the Ochrana, the czar's secret police, had arrested and tortured him on vague charges of harboring suspicious opinions, an arrest that pushed him into a life of subversive action that had him sentenced to ten years of hard labor in Siberia. Those experiences shaped him into a determined revolutionary who was especially dangerous because, as he realizes on his escape from Siberia, he has no fear: "On the way he made a remarkable discovery about himself: he had lost the ability to feel fear. Something had happened in his mind, as if a switch was closed. He could think of nothing that could frighten him. If hungry, he would steal; if chased, he would hide; if threatened, he would kill. There was nothing he wanted. Nothing could hurt him anymore. Love, pride, desire and compassion were forgotten emotions" (34). This attitude makes Kschessinsky a formidable opponent. His decision to go to England to murder Orlov puts him into the role of the spy who enters a hostile territory and must escape detection and carry out a difficult mission. A reader might be ready to sympathize with a character like Kschessinsky because he has suffered unjustly, but the reader cannot be comfortable with Kschessinsky's thoroughly amoral behavior as he steals at will and manipulates people as needed.

Kschessinsky undergoes character changes in response to discoveries he makes during the novel. He interrupts his first assassination attempt when he sees his old love in the carriage and learns to feel again love and a desire for life when he discovers that he has a daughter. He never abandons his plan to assassinate Orlov, but he becomes a more interesting and complicated character. At the end of the novel Kschessinsky has an opportunity to perform a heroic action, and the reader is likely to be touched by his unflinching devotion to his daughter.

Kschessinsky's love for Lydia, which led to his original arrest by the Ochrana, interferes with his first assassination attempt. He and the reader learn from Lydia that her father had ordered Kschessinsky arrested in Russia when he discovered that she was having an affair with a commoner. She had struck a deal with her father, who agreed to release the man if she married the young English lord, Stephen Walden, who had just become interested in her. Lydia's overwhelming passion had driven her into this terrible situation; compensating for her deeply passionate nature becomes the dominant feature of the rest of her life. The extent of Lydia's passionate nature is suggested early in the novel when the mere mention of a "young Russian" reminds her of a lover she had nineteen years before and causes such a physical reaction that she is momentarily shaken. This suggestion that she has a secret and passionate past is surprising to the reader at first because up to that point Lydia has appeared to be the epitome of a proper, disciplined Victorian lady. A memory triggered in her husband suggests that she does not have much passion for him. In her household she behaves like an aristocrat, the station to which she was born in Russia and into which she married. Her rigid behavior, especially toward her daughter, suggests that her self-control is actually a defense against her passionate nature. The conflict between these two aspects creates some of the conflicts that shape the novel. Lydia discovers that she is still capable of extraordinary passion when Kschessinsky kisses her during a surprise visit to her house; coming to terms with this passion, while trying to keep it a secret, creates the tension she faces throughout the novel.

The balance to Lydia's passionate nature is Stephen Walden's controlled and steady certainty about his world and how it should be ordered. He is deeply disappointed that he has not been able to win Lydia's love, but his feelings are located firmly within a framework of aristocratic values and attitudes. Although he argued with his father while his father was alive, time and experience have made him aware that those differences might have arisen from the fact that the two were very much alike. He comes to appreciate his father's virtues and attitudes even more as he sees their aristocratic lifestyle and dominant place in society slipping in the face of democratic government and ideals. The reader develops some degree of sympathy for him because he moderates his behavior. That moderation translates into something like the decency that Follett heroes always have. Walden earns his place as a hero because of his bravery, his steadfastness, and his willingness to do his duty even when he is not absolutely committed to the cause. These are the virtues of a domestic hero rather than the usual hero of a thriller, but Follett seems to be interested in exploring the possibilities of heroic action within more confined definitions of heroism, and Walden seems to be a test of those possibilities. He certainly qualifies as the amateur brought into action by the call of duty. Indeed, the novel opens with repeated solicitations of, first, Churchill and then the king to involve him in the action. This willingness to serve when called upon endears Walden to the reader and balances against his unsympathetic conservative and aristocratic positions. His actions and responses to change make him an engaging hero by the end of the novel when he joins Kschessinsky in the rescue of Charlotte.

The novel opens with Charlotte Walden, the other main character, as an eighteen-year-old who is innocent and childish to a fault. Her mother asks a maid where Charlotte and her cousin are. The subsequent bustle about not being able to keep track of her indicates that Charlotte's mother treats her like a child. The reader's first glimpse of Charlotte is in a conversation with her cousin about the facts of life. The terms they use are surprisingly childish for young women their age. Their extreme naiveté introduces the novel's concern with the Victorian propensity to keep women from knowledge about the world. Indeed, Charlotte's determination to become more worldly becomes a plot device and thematic vehicle as well. The reader learns early that she is headstrong and passionate as her mother was when young and that she has a feel for serious and important matters that is lacking in her cousin, Belinda. Belinda also grows up during the novel and manages to gain some knowledge of the world, but it is by contrast limited to fashion and she has no interest in the issues that compel Charlotte's attention. The revelation that Kschessinsky is actually Charlotte's father suggests that some of her commitment to causes and to global concerns such as justice and women's rights grows out of the passionate nature she inherited from her parents. Kschessinsky initiates Charlotte's education after he rescues her from a riot following a suffragette march. Charlotte had participated in that demonstration as a cultural and political innocent and is almost destroyed in the outburst of hate and violence it provokes. Kschessinsky brings her into adult awareness with his patient explanations. Charlotte benefits as well from Walden's attempts to help her understand her adult world. He succeeds not so much in terms of the information he offers Charlotte as in the balance and patience he demonstrates in how to handle it. The impulse to act upon new information that Charlotte seems to have inherited from her biological father is tempered by the equanimity that she learns from her adoptive father.

Plot Development

The plot of *The Man from St. Petersburg* consists of a straightforward action with one very wide detour. The main action is the decision by Kschessinsky to assassinate Prince Orlov and so destroy the negotiations between Britain and Russia. That plot line is established in the first chapter and gives the novel focus through the third chapter, when Kschessinsky, having laid his trap for Orlov, opens the carriage door and prepares to shoot the prince. The woman's cry that opens the fourth chapter paralyzes him and creates a delay, causing the attempt to fail and enabling Walden to wound him and chase him away with a ceremonial sword. Kschessinsky's recognition of Lydia complicates the plot, although it does not deter him from quickly resuming his schemes. The complication grows to include an antagonism between Kschessinsky and Walden that is fueled by their implicit rivalry over Lydia and ultimately their claims on Charlotte. Kschessinsky recognizes that he cannot reclaim Lydia, and he uses her information to plan another attempt on Orlov's life. When that plan is foiled by Walden, Kschessinsky begins his third attempt to kill Orlov, and that plan is interrupted by his discovery that

Charlotte is his daughter. He pauses in his planning long enough to establish a bond with her and to realize that he now has something to live for. He then returns to the plan for the assassination but with the slight hope that he will survive and be able to retain enough of Charlotte's affection to make his future inviting. The final chapters, like the ending of many spy thrillers, resolve the action in a chase. The first part of the chase, the physical chasing of Kschessinsky from London to Walden Hall, resembles the action of other Follett novels. However, the last steps in the chase occur inside the house, a confined space that creates tension with the hunter and the quarry only rooms apart from each other. This action within a restricted space reflects Follett's interest in domestic action as the material for exciting stories and his experiments with the conventions of plotting in thrillers.

The action of *The Man from St. Petersburg* takes on a special dimension of suspense because the setting of the novel begins with a secret diplomatic mission. Europe just before World War I was characterized by complicated and shifting political alliances accompanied by endless plots and schemes. Thus, the very setting engages the reader's interest in suspense and action. The reader knows that much is riding on this action, and the plot is all the more engaging because of the complexities of the setting.

The novel ends on a melodramatic note as the aristocratic ancestral home goes up in flames, the assassin shoots his intended victim, Charlotte's two "fathers" work together to rescue her from the fire despite their personal and political animosities, and the assassin dies after making a selfless and heroic gesture for his daughter's sake. All the loose ends of the plot are resolved, even the treaty between Russia and England. The extravagant heroism of the rescue of Charlotte and Kschessinsky's self-sacrifice is balanced by Churchill's cold and cynical political decision to create a fictional account of Orlov's death in order to save the treaty.

Thematic Issues

The Man from St. Petersburg focuses on the desire to create a more perfect government. The story presents a range of governments from the feudal Russian aristocracy still exercising absolute power over people to the modern British democracy, which elects representatives to exercise power in the name of the people. The career of Feliks Kschessinsky por-

trays the conflict between the czar and the revolutionary forces determined to replace the aristocracy with an egalitarian government. The
British government portrays a compromise between aristocracy and democracy that has avoided a revolution but has not yet achieved a fully
just government. Kschessinsky's revolutionary opposition is mirrored in
the activities of the British suffragettes, suggesting that working for a
more perfect government is an ongoing task in human history. The novel
suggests that the urge to develop ideal forms of government be accompanied by the balance needed to pursue personal and social ideals as
well. Charlotte's involvement with the suffragette movement offers a series of reminders that democratic governments must be careful to include
all citizens in their processes.

Charlotte's faulty education reveals the oppressive attitudes toward
women that lead to their exclusion from political structures. The theme
of the inadequate education of women is introduced when Charlotte and
Belinda steal two books from the library to find out how babies are born.
The only two books they can find that deal with sex are an antiseptic-
sounding medical text and a poorly written pornographic novel, both of
which suggest the inability of the culture to articulate its own feelings
about sexuality and marriage. Lydia has explicitly kept Charlotte ignorant of anything to do with sex because of Lydia's own memory of her
passion for Kschessinsky, and so she enacts the common Victorian belief
that passion must be repressed and ignored to avoid the trouble that it
was perceived to cause.

The novel suggests that the nineteenth-century understanding of human feelings was hampered by a sense of people torn between two opposing forces, the urge to work hard to make the world a better place
and the urge to pursue destructive passions. Charlotte thinks at one
point that she feels like "Dr. Jekyl and Mr. Hyde," reminding the reader
of one of the many nineteenth-century stories about personalities split
between good and evil. Lydia's sense of herself parallels her experience
both as a young girl and as an adult as being split between a person of
deep and dangerous passions and a completely controlled person who
acts virtuously at all times. The novel suggests that happiness is best
found in some middle ground. Stephen Walden has strong convictions
and deep feelings balanced with a sense of patience and duty, and these
moderating impulses enable him to act in terms other than absolute control or complete abandonment. The cruelty of the czarist police, who
ruined Kschessinsky's early life, and the rigid social codes that drove
Lydia to adopt a false role for almost twenty years show that absolute

power in any arena twists the lives of good people. Both Kschessinsky and Lydia are driven to obsessive behaviors, even if their lives take different directions. The political and social decisions that create anarchists and reactionaries create effects far beyond their immediate spheres of influence. The destructive consequences of absolute commitments either way suggest the attractiveness of virtues such as Walden's.

Literary Devices

The novel begins with an epigraph from Graham Greene: "One can't love humanity. One can only love people." The words alert the reader to look for people in the novel who talk about loving humanity but fail to love individuals. Kschessinsky seeks to establish justice and love on a universal basis through revolutionary change. Walden's aristocratic order is equally distanced from caring about individual people and is dramatized by Lydia's failure to know the names of her servants. Charlotte suggests this charge when she accuses her father of failing to take care of Annie, the pregnant servant who was driven from Walden Hall. Charlotte is both engaged by generalized theories of human nature and human history and responsive to individual people. The changes in Charlotte during the novel suggest that both impulses are present in her, and the Epilogue outlines both commitment to causes and love of individuals throughout her long career.

Perhaps the most notable reflection of the epigraph is Kschessinsky's response to his discovery that Lydia has become Lady Walden. He reviews his life after he was snatched from her and finds some consolation in his commitment to his cause: "His love was not for people, it was for *the* people. His compassion was for striving peasants in general, and sick children and frightened soldiers and crippled miners in general. He hated nobody in particular: just all princes, all landlords, all capitalists and all generals" (123). This example of distanced and generalized hate and love appears to have been created by years of extraordinary suffering and deprivation, so the credibility of the principle is undercut by the unusual conditions that produced it. The reader suspects that the recent discovery of his lost love might bring him to abandon his alienation and hate. The epigraph and its echoes in the novel introduce a thematic concern about the ways that people generalize too quickly to principles of love and hate from their own limited experiences. The novel shows mature generosity and respect for others as the qualities that can change the world for the better. The experiences depicted in the novel suggest that both aristocrats and Communists would be better off under a system that keeps people in close conversation and away from prejudices caused by class, money, and power.

LIE DOWN WITH LIONS

The title *Lie Down with Lions* reflects the novel's setting in the Five Lions Valley of Afghanistan and the fact that some of the main characters embrace the people of that valley while others betray them. It also offers a wry comment on the sexual intimacy shared one night by Jane Lambert, the novel's heroine, and Ellis Thaler, the American CIA agent who comes to the valley and whose long blond hair reminds the Afghans of a lion's mane. The night they spend together becomes a central moment in the book because it marks her commitment to Ellis, which has to be final in a censorious society such as Afghanistan, and it is interrupted by a surprise attack from the Russian troops searching for him. The title thus asks the reader to think about the complex political personal and social relationships in the novel.

The note at the beginning of the novel somewhat coyly announces that the events described are based in history but not on specific events. The war between the Russian-supported Afghan government and rebellious Afghan tribesmen had not even ended when Ken Follett wrote this novel, so readers do not come to the book with the same kind of certainty about historical events that they have brought to previous novels. But as in Follett's earlier works, the action is set in a crucial point in a historical event, and the actions of the central figure make a big difference in the outcome of the war.

Point of View

The narrator of *Lie Down with Lions* introduces the reader immediately to the world of international espionage and murder, including the thoughts, motives, and histories of the major and minor characters engaged in the schemes and negotiations in Paris of 1981. This narrator's omniscient perspective assures the reader that he or she has access to all information needed to follow the actions of the story and the motives and decisions of the characters. The narrator has no role in the action and maintains an impersonal and distanced perspective.

The point of view shifts from character to character as needed, generally chapter by chapter. One chapter is seen from the perspective of a single character and the next chapter from that of another. Because this narrative pattern introduces the evolving awareness and involvement of each character, it gives the reader a sense of the action as slow and deliberate, but the multiple perspectives eventually create a feeling of suspense and tension. The action in Afghanistan is seen primarily through Jane's perspective and offers many details about village life and the daily lives of women and children. Jane's strong central presence gives a distinctly feminine character to the virtues and the wisdom that distinguish this novel among Follett's other novels and the genre of spy thrillers.

Character Development

The action of the novel centers on three characters: Ellis Thaler, a CIA agent working undercover in Paris; Jane Lambert, a bright and beautiful Englishwoman working as a translator in Paris, who is friendly with a number of local revolutionaries; and Jean-Pierre, a French doctor and confirmed socialist already committed to working for the Communists. Only sketchy backgrounds are given for each character: Ellis has a thirteen-year-old daughter who lives with his ex-wife and her husband and he tries to keep in touch with her. His parents live in a middle-class suburb in New Jersey and he gets along well with them. Jane grew up in an upper-middle-class family in Hampshire, England, and is interested in making a difference in the world. Jean-Pierre's father, a former Resistance fighter and persecuted socialist, influenced him to work for the Communists in Paris and then in Afghanistan. Ellis had pursued Jane initially to take advantage of her contacts but has fallen in love with her by the opening of the novel. He tells his CIA supervisor that he intends to ask her to marry him, although he never gets that chance because Jean-Pierre reveals to Jane that Ellis is an agent just before the Communists attack Ellis's apartment. Jane is furious at the news because she feels betrayed, Ellis has no opportunity to explain himself, and the separation caused by the attack leaves Jane in the arms of Jean-Pierre.

From the beginning of the novel Ellis is presented as a dependable and talented person. His work in Paris leads to the capture of two of the most important suppliers of terrorists, and the reader's observation of him under pressure, that of physical attack and that of trying to balance his real feelings for Jane with his duties as a covert agent, leads to a positive attachment to him as a character. He is on the side of the good guys, he succeeds well, and he is as honest and sensitive as he can be under the circumstances. Jane makes an equally good impression on the reader. She is forthright and honest with herself when she thinks about her relationship with Ellis. Men fall in love with her with unusual regularity, but she takes no special pride in that and commits herself to only one person at a time. By contrast, the novel presents Jean-Pierre as unattractive from the very beginning. He wishes that Ellis would be hit by a bus so that he could have a chance with Jane. He thinks about seducing a medical student who is having problems with her studies; his lack of real interest in her problem coupled with his calculations on seducing her identifies him as selfish and deceitful. His interest in Jane, which the reader knows to be genuine, takes on a possessive and mean character throughout the novel.

The events of the novel reveal Jean-Pierre to be every bit the snake that the opening chapters suggest. He takes advantage of his position as a doctor who presumably has come to save the Afghan fighters and their families and betrays them to the Russians. He misjudges his Russian allies and finds himself treated badly by them when he does not deliver what he has promised. When he does catch up with Jane at the end of the chase, he finds that slapping her is his most pleasurable response, and he seems to look forward to doing more of it as soon as he regains complete control over her. The character development of Jean-Pierre goes from that of a somewhat unsympathetic person to a despicable one.

Jane grows in the reader's estimation chapter by chapter. In Afghanistan she makes herself a useful part of the effort to aid the Afghans even if her advice to the women about birth control is less welcome than some of her other services. The reader's first sight of her in Afghanistan is when she saves the life of a boy injured by a land mine. She figures out that Jean-Pierre is a spy and smashes his radio to keep him from betraying any more convoys, and she uses her sexual attractiveness and her knowledge of local customs to influence an Afghan leader to keep a convoy out of harm's way. From the reader's point of view, she is more than generous in her attempts to keep her marriage and family together, and she makes clear and good decisions when she recognizes that she and Jean-Pierre can never be reconciled. When she has to begin a difficult journey, she proves herself the equal of the men she accompanies. With her infant in a sling, she handles a gun and shoots Jean-Pierre when it becomes necessary as she and Ellis escape.

Plot Development

Lie Down with Lions uses the Russian involvement in Afghanistan to present three spy stories: Ellis Thaler's capture of the terrorists in Paris at the beginning of the novel, Jean-Pierre's spying on the Afghan rebel activity in the Five Lions Valley, and Ellis's mission to unite the Afghan rebels against the Russian troops. Each of these actions requires the spy to go over into hostile territory, which offers a number of suspense-generating situations. The initial spy story about Ellis in Paris is more useful for character development and for setting up the main plot, although it also puts the reader right into the surprise and tension of the spy's world. The other two spy actions overlap in time. Jean-Pierre's spying on the Afghan tribesmen ends when he leaves his cover behind to betray the council of rebel leaders. Ellis's actual spying lasts only a short while longer, since Jean-Pierre reveals Ellis's presence to the Russians. The last six chapters are devoted to the chase, with Jane and Ellis trying to escape and Jean-Pierre and Anatoly, the Russian soldier in charge, engaged in determined and effective pursuit. Thus, the plot structure offers the tension and suspense of spying, discovery, and chase actions throughout the novel in three increasingly complex versions.

The novel offers a subplot—Jane's attempt to find a place for herself in the society of the valley, a difficult task given the rigid and extensive differences between the Afghan people and their Western visitors. Both Jean-Pierre and Ellis connect with their hosts: Jean-Pierre offers medical help and Ellis provides weapons and organizational strategy. But Jane, partly owing to her pregnancy and the birth of her daughter, becomes more integrated into the life of the village, and her connections with the people are deeper and more personal. She develops an understanding of Afghan culture and both respects and uses it in responding to daily events as well as emergencies. She succeeds in earning a measure of respect from the Afghan women and from some of the men. Her presence in the village establishes a basis for further understanding and friendship between the cultures.

The main plot ends with a flurry of reversals. Ellis and Jane get a good start on their flight but are betrayed by the mullah, the local Muslim religious leader. Then they gain advantages by making extraordinary sacrifices as they travel, only to lose those advantages when a guide betrays them. Mohammed, the leader of the village, gives up his life to gain them some time on the trail but not enough time to throw the Russians off entirely. As the pursuers close in, Ellis sets a trap that will blow up a hillside on them, but Jane refuses to detonate the explosive at the critical moment and they are captured. In captivity they seem defeated, but at a critical moment Ellis and Jane overpower their captors and escape for good in a Russian helicopter. These dramatic reversals provide all the excitement the reader of a spy thriller could want. The tension and suspense build up in the final chapters and then are suddenly released with Jane and Ellis's escape. A final chapter, set a year later, pulls together the last few details of their lives and establishes them in a happily-ever-after mode.

Thematic Issues

The two main themes of *Lie Down with Lions* suggest that the Russian involvement in the Afghan war parallels the American experience in Vietnam and that women succeed better than men in international relations and have a responsibility to press their solutions on the policy makers. The comparison between the two national involvements underscores the stupidity of powerful industrial nations waging war. Despite the mistakes of the United States in Vietnam, the Soviet Union follows the same path in Afghanistan. Ellis's service in Vietnam underscores the parallel, as does Jane's thinking about the effects of the war on the Afghan villagers: "Jane feared that the Russians would make this evacuation their policy—that, unable to defeat the guerrillas, they would try to destroy the communities within which the guerrillas lived, as the Americans had in Vietnam, by carpet-bombing whole areas of the countryside, so that the Five Lions Valley would become an uninhabited wasteland, and Mohammed and Zahara and Rabia would join the homeless, stateless, aimless occupants of the camps" (96). This comparison suggests that the Russian actions will be as futile as the American war in Vietnam. Masud makes the same comparison later on in a conversation with Ellis, who then uses the information to develop an understanding about how Masud can defeat the Russians. The novel suggests that continued Russian engagement in Afghanistan can benefit no one and certainly will cause serious damage to all parties involved. Follett regularly reminds the reader that the Afghans are fighting for their liberty and their homes, aims that are designed to elicit sympathy for the Afghans and antipathy to the Russian presence.

The second major theme, the superior sensibility of women in war, builds on the absurdity of the Russian war in Afghanistan and perhaps of all wars pursued by industrial powers. The theme appears first when Jane tells Jean-Pierre that the most valuable thing Westerners can give to Afghan people is information about access to the benefits of modern life, which is much more valuable than medicine and drugs given to one opponent or another. The argument is certainly true for weapons as well. The reader recognizes the strength of Jane's convictions about the importance of family over war when she tries to persuade Jean-Pierre to preserve their family by leaving Afghanistan. She also introduces a dissenting voice on the importance of Masud's winning the war when she reminds Ellis that as a Muslim fundamentalist Masud will clamp down on women as soon as he gets into power and that the restrictions on women will be followed by restrictions on other groups in disfavor with Muslim law and custom.

Jane makes the connection between war and gender explicit after the Russians return to Banda to find Ellis and kill the young village boy Mousa and the wounded guerrilla fighters. Jane tells Ellis that men are bloody, suggesting that men use violence quickly and with enthusiasm to settle conflicts and that Mousa died emulating a model taught to him by his father, not his mother. Ellis seems puzzled by her statement, although he does not argue with her. Jane acts on these convictions during the escape at the end when she refuses to trigger the blast that will kill the Russian pursuers because their party includes five young men. When Ellis asks why she failed to detonate the explosive, she explains, "Because they have mothers" (353). Her actions throughout the novel offer not only an alternative view on war but a credible example of actions motivated by deep convictions. Her stand does not resolve the conflicts in the novel, and indeed, when Jean-Pierre beats her after she is captured, she responds with violence and kills him to save herself and her child from a life of brutality. Her concern for peace attains a level of importance unusual in a novel focused on wars and espionage. Follett has a history of creating strong and inventive women characters, but Jane Lambert is certainly the strongest up to this point in his career. Her role at the center of the novel's action reinforces the theme of the importance of feminine perspectives.

Literary Devices

Lie Down with Lions makes good use of metaphor, simile, and poetry. Early in the novel both Jean-Pierre and Ellis repeatedly use the metaphor of being "run over by a bus," suggesting the constant risk that spies live with. The icy Five Lions River "boiled through the ravines and flashed past the wheat fields in a headlong dash for the faraway lowlands" (47), creating a vivid sensory impression of the river. The naming of the donkey after Margaret Thatcher reflects Jane's wit but also suggests Follett's willingness to play with the political reference points of the novel. At times, the narrator offers straightforward similes such as the comparison between the Washington CIA agent and a shark (84) or the comparison of the Afghan fighters with lions (85). At times, the narrator drops the explicit comparison and offers a metaphor such as the following: "Oh, we will catch him [Masud]. He knows the hunt is in full cry, so he covers his tracks. But the hounds have his scent, and he cannot elude us forever—we are so many, and so strong, and our blood is up" (123). The extended metaphor, the same metaphor Follett used in *Triple*, serves as a measure of the speaker's (Anatoly) state of mind and identifies the kind of chase at hand.

In chapter 5, which brings Ellis back into the story, Follett uses quotes from two poems, a change of pace in a novel and especially in a spy thriller. The first quote, from W. H. Auden, suggests that Ellis is more literate and sensitive than the average spy. The poignancy of the verse when applied to Ellis's own situation strikes the reader as touching. The second quote is from a Rudyard Kipling poem that Ellis quotes to discomfort the CIA operative, whom he does not like very much. The stanza catches the CIA person off guard because it reminds him uncomfortably that the fields of his operation are dangerous and brutal, and he had not intended to be bested by his lunch partner in quite that manner. The agent recovers by dismissing the stanza as part of Ellis's cover in Paris, and the conversation moves on. Ellis's poetic bent, however, reveals the complexity of his mind, his independence from the CIA, and his ability to adopt a unique and engaging response to situations.

A Feminist Approach to *The Man from St. Petersburg* and *Lie Down with Lions*

Feminist literary criticism can be traced to initial protestations that masculine evaluations of works by and about women were unfair. The larger discussion about the place of women in culture and history that has evolved during the past thirty years has led to a systematic criticism of literary works based on convictions about the importance of feminist perspectives. Feminist criticism argues that male-dominated Western civilization has regularly oppressed women by denying them access to political, cultural, economic, and artistic life and insisting that they define themselves solely in terms of their relationship to men. Feminist criticism calls for change, reform, or revolution in political, economic, and cultural spheres.

Feminist critics use an attack on patriarchy as a starting point for an elaboration and articulation of the reality and experiences that women share, which may differ considerably from men's. Because any dominant ideology presents its view of the world as natural and inevitable, feminists must articulate the alternative reality that shapes their perspectives, their understanding of the world, and their personal experiences. Some of that effort redefines the characteristics of patriarchal culture. Feminists stress the importance of intuition and feelings to operate successfully and productively in the world. The world they posit may be close to or far away from commonly accepted norms, but this vision offers an alternative to patriarchal culture for both men and women to consider.

Feminist literary critics have benefitted from the insights of feminist writers about the ways in which language is shaped by gender. Feminists have pointed to the many terms that implicitly equate valuable qualities with masculine experience ("virile") and dangerous or suspect qualities with women's experience ("hysterical"). Feminists call for women to write and develop a set of linguistic practices that take their shape and structure from experiences that are distinctly female. These exhortations emphasize the patriarchal culture's repression of women's bodies and women's language and suggest that emancipation of each may be through the development of the other. Early feminists also noted that women had been denied a history of their own and so needed to develop that history. Their recognition that the oppression of women had taken place at these basic levels instilled a sense that a major recovery project was needed before women could articulate their needs and change the future.

Feminist literary criticism studies the images of women in literary works written by both men and women. Feminist critics often find that women are depicted according to received stereotypes rather than out of understanding of the reality of their lives. These analyses expose the patriarchal domination of literature and enable the reader to recognize similar gender-defined writing. A reader influenced by a feminist analysis might also work to change attitudes toward women and the work of women. Thus, a feminist literary analysis adds to the body of knowledge about the connections between gender and culture, adds to a reader's repertoire of reading strategies in approaching other texts, and increases the adoption of attitudes more hospitable to women. Other literary criticism has the potential for all these functions; feminist literary criticism incorporates these elements as basic aims.

Some feminist literary criticism reads mainstream works as embodiments of the contradictions in values and perspectives derived from a male-oriented culture. The contrary attitude that feminists have to develop in order to articulate their experiences in a patriarchal culture carry over into the reading of literary works and produce analyses that offer insights likely to be quite at odds with traditional explanations. These contrary readings, like deconstructive readings, locate the places in the text where the contradictions inherent in oppressive culture, perhaps unseen by the writer and male readers, undercut the intended strategies and structures. Other feminist literary critics identify both role models for women and feminist concerns and so use the discussion as an occasion for raising the reader's consciousness.

Set in England in 1914, a time when the male-dominated society of the nineteenth century had reached its highest development, *The Man from St. Petersburg* illuminates the problem of this society and presents patriarchy as a system full of problems and contradictions. One of the turning points is a suffragette march that is broken up with brute force by police and privately hired thugs. In addition, the novel clearly supports the development and decisions of Charlotte as a strong-minded and determined woman. Charlotte pursues her impulses and intuitions in deciding to discover the goals of the suffragette movement and then steps forward to join the march when she decides that she agrees with them. Endowed with a sharp intelligence, she emerges from a headstrong girl into a person with clear and admirable convictions and the will to pursue them.

But despite its support of women and its dissatisfaction with a patriarchal society, the novel stops short of condemning this society and might not meet the expectations of a feminist critic.

The ambiguity about partriarchal structures is evident in the treatment of Lydia. Her life as a sexually repressed woman appears to reflect nineteenth-century attitudes toward women and marriage. She articulates her fears about her own dark and passionate drives and attempts to protect her daughter from exposure to any similar experiences. Yet the extraordinary acceptance and love of her husband, Walden, is at odds with typical nineteenth-century attitudes toward women. He offers a positive model of possible male-female relationships. The moment in the story when Lydia buckles under to patriarchy and reactionary politics by agreeing to marry him might also be read as a triumph of her making the decision to trade her marriage choice for the life of her lover and the security of the child she is carrying. By saving Kschessinsky and having his baby, she steps outside the strict requirements of patriarchal aristocracy. Although she is forced into a life of absolute respectability, her revolutionary nature is at least partially vindicated in her daughter's independence of mind and the continued revolutionary activity of her lover. Thus, her twenty years of repressed sexuality might be a measure of her mettle and her determination to honor her bargain. It is not that her career is something different from what it appears at first glance to a reader; rather, a feminist critic sees that version of her career as only one aspect of Lydia's character.

The Man from St. Petersburg posits a complicated historical question— What caused World War I?—a question that is thrown into relief by feminist concerns. Kschessinsky's work as a Russian revolutionary reminds the reader of the deep tensions in Europe in 1914 caused by the reactionary aristocratic system and the implicitly repressive capitalistic system. These repressive forces create the context within which another important revolutionary force, the movement to give women the vote, develops. This movement threatens the status quo of European patriarchy because it reaches into the households of the highest levels of the aristocracy. Charlotte's attraction to the suffragette movement suggests a power that arises both from her genetic inheritance and from her upbringing. She is responsive both to her parents' predisposition to freedom and independence and to the conflicts in values and assumptions embedded in the world beyond the aristocracy.

A feminist critic might integrate some apparently minor details into the larger concerns of the novel. The episode in which Charlotte and her cousin, Belinda, pursue their curiosity about sex by ferreting out from Walden's library a copy of what sounds like a section of a physiological textbook and a turgid pornographic novel looks like a character-defining interlude. A feminist might point out that the episode reminds the reader of the ignorance that was part of the culture's means of keeping women in servitude. A similar episode in which Charlotte insists that the household take in Annie, a former servant who shows up at the gates pregnant and abandoned, reveals Charlotte's spontaneous and kind nature. But it also points out the limited range of choices open to women in that society and the cruelty with which society enforced its gender and class codes. Finally, the novel's closing perspective, which projects Charlotte's life into the late twentieth century, emphasizes her experiences and the wisdom she accumulates in a long and successful life in a still male-dominated society. This image is expressed in feminist terms. The Epilogue traces her active involvement in politics and her success as the "leading English translator of nineteenth-century Russian fiction" (342). The focus on her continued passion for political and gender issues emphasizes the sustaining force these passions can be: "[Charlotte] is not all memories though. She denounces the Communist Party of the Soviet Union for giving socialism a bad name. If you tell her that Mrs. Thatcher is no feminist, she will say that Brezhnev is no socialist" (342). The novel suggests that Charlotte's life and career embody the struggles and the hopes for feminist political and social agendas.

A feminist critic of *Lie Down with Lions* might focus on Jane Lambert, a strong character and, for the men in the novel, a highly desirable woman. A feminist reading enhances her strengths and power and integrates them into the concerns of the novel. Jane's actions encourage the reading of the novel as an important feminist statement. Jane refuses to detonate the explosion that Ellis had set to stop their pursuers because, looking down on the young Afghan soldiers in the pursuing group, she refuses to kill another mother's son. Jane articulates this feminist viewpoint earlier in the novel when she challenges the men's responses to a young boy's death as a heroic act. She insists that the mourners see the waste of the boy's life as he tried to act out the heroic values he had learned from the men in his life. She takes a big risk in opposing male-dominated society's deeply held values; she takes an even bigger risk when she acts on her convictions, refuses to detonate the trap, and so enables the pursuers to capture her, her lover, and her baby. In supporting Jane's action, which violates the reader's expectations of the way people act during a chase, the novel takes a distinctive feminist turn that makes sense only in terms of woman-centered values. The feminist reading of the novel enables the reader to see that the novel succeeds despite its unconventional handling of an important convention.

8

The Pillars of the Earth
(1989) and
A Dangerous Fortune
(1993)

A saga promises a reader a look at a complex historical moment by focusing on a family and the ways its own history reflects and is shaped by the events and forces occurring around it. Because readers have their own family histories as points of reference, they find the focus of a saga familiar and an easy entrée to the complex historical forces shaping the family. Sagas teach readers about the values and patterns that shape history and identify the admirable and contemptible behavior of people caught up in those historical moments. *The Pillars of the Earth* follows the fortunes of a family touched by the shift from the feudal system and an agricultural economy to an early version of the nation-state and the emergence of capitalism as a buffer between people and both political and ecclesiastical tyranny. *A Dangerous Fortune* looks at tyranny in politics and society once capitalism has triumphed and money becomes the new source of authority in nineteenth-century England. Both novels use the saga to focus on crucial moments in history when values and traditions were established that are still important to readers today.

THE PILLARS OF THE EARTH

The saga requires a sense of communal history. That history is embodied in this novel in the building of a medieval cathedral. Ken Follett had an interest in cathedrals and their architecture for much of his adult life and had proposed a book focused on cathedrals to a publisher in 1976. *The Pillars of the Earth* represents his decision that he was ready to write the kind of big book that the subject of cathedrals seemed to require. He had gained extensive knowledge about cathedrals and about life in the twelfth century and used it to give *Pillars* a strong sense of historical accuracy. The Middle Ages was a time when both church and state recognized a common source of history and law in the Roman Catholic Church. This social and political unity is epitomized in the building of a cathedral, because it requires the extraordinary resources of time, energy, and money that only a whole society over three or more generations could pull together. Cathedrals rose to celebrate the glory of God by offering an occasion for all his creatures to work together and then to worship together. The building of the cathedral itself would call into being many extraordinary family stories. In *The Pillars of the Earth*, family history is a vehicle for examining the important transition in Western life from the unified theocentric vision of the Middle Ages to the fragmented and individualized sense of human life that characterizes the modern world.

To set up the special historical moment that characterizes so many of his novels, Follett begins with an epigraph from a history of medieval England by A. L. Poole titled *From Domesday Book to Magna Carta*:

> On the night of 25 November 1120 the White Ship set out for England and foundered off Barfleur with all hands save one. . . . The vessel was latest thing in marine transport, fitted with all the devices known to the shipbuilder of the time. . . . The notoriety of this wreck is due to the very large number of distinguished persons on board; beside the king's son and heir, there were two royal bastards, several earls and barons, and most of the royal household . . . its historical significance is that it left Henry without an obvious heir . . . its ultimate result was the disputed succession and the period of anarchy which followed Henry's death. (7)

This epigraph asks the reader to think about a moment in English history that created the first English martyr, St. Thomas à Becket, and prepared for Canterbury Cathedral to be the foremost ecclesiastical seat in England and later the chief see of the Church of England. Although the epigraph's relevance is not immediately apparent to the reader, the action of the novel ultimately shows the connection between the shipwreck and both the immediate fortunes of one fictional family and the larger patterns of history depicted in the book.

Point of View

Like Follett's other novels, *Pillars* uses an omniscient narrator who knows all the events and thoughts connected with each character and tells them to the reader as the story demands. The Prologue relates a hanging that takes place in 1123. The sudden entrance into a world of crime and violence gets the novel off to a quick start, but it also adds an element of mystery because the narrator merely describes the scene and omits any explanation of prior events that led up to it or introduction to the thoughts and feelings of the witnesses. The first chapter of Part 1, 1135–1136, shifts abruptly to another story and offers no connection to the Prologue, leaving the reader with the expectation that a further explanation will be coming.

In the body of the novel, the narrator's perspective expands to include the thoughts and feelings of the characters. This device creates fully developed characters. The point of view shifts from one character to another in any given chapter. At times the narrator offers accounts of the same event from different points of view. These accounts sometimes overlap. Often this multiple perspective prepares the reader for an important dimension of the plot. For instance, the beatings inflicted by the boy Alfred on his younger stepbrother seem like nothing to Alfred, but their memory takes on more importance when the reader learns of the deep resentment they caused in the stepbrother. These early conflicts play out later in important detail. At times point of view is used to indicate changes in time or place. In the expansive framework of the saga the reader needs to keep a running account of the time frames in order to follow the action and its scope.

The narrator offers some suggestions early on as to why the reader should pay close attention to the many architectural details that form a significant part of the novel. The narrator points out that Agnes, the wife of Tom the Builder, resents his interest in building cathedrals, especially when working on houses instead could provide a comfortable living for her and their children: "She could not comprehend the irresistible attraction of building a cathedral: the absorbing complexity of organization, the intellectual challenge of the calculations, the sheer size of the walls, and the breathtaking beauty and grandeur of the finished building" (23). In offering an explanation of the attractions of cathedrals, the narrator provides the reader with some idea of why paying close attention to the details of cathedral building is important and why a lack of interest in such details might place the reader in the same category as the materialistic and comfort-bound Agnes.

Character Development

The two most prominent and admirable characters in the novel are women, an extraordinary feature of a novel set in a time when women had no legal status and relied on men for cultural recognition. The first woman the reader meets is the young girl who utters the dramatic curse depicted in the Prologue, whom later events reveal as Ellen. Ellen appears with her son, Jack, out of the woods in a mysterious and, for the family of Tom the Builder, miraculous fashion. That appearance serves both plot and theme in the development of the novel. Throughout the novel Ellen is associated with the wild and mysterious aspects of life, and her strong will and unyielding sense of right and wrong make her a constant critic of a society that regards its theological learning as the source of order and explanation for everything under the sun. Ellen has lived in the woods with her son after the hanging of her lover, and her reemergence is occasioned by her meeting with Tom the Builder as he and his starving family wander in the woods. After they bury Tom's wife, Agnes, Ellen enters society again because of her attachment to Tom, but her skepticism regarding the authority and virtue of the church and the aristocracy makes her a tentative resident of society at best.

Aliena, the daughter of a dispossessed earl, Robert, becomes the major force in the action of the novel and almost a partner in the building of the cathedral. She attracts the reader's attention at first because, contrary to law and tradition, she refuses to marry the young lord, William Hamleigh, who has sought her hand. Such independence may have been unusual in the Middle Ages, but it is not unusual in fiction about the medieval period. Her defiance has the immediate effect of stopping the construction of the house being built for her and thus putting Tom the Builder out of work and sending him and his family on the wandering that leads him to Ellen in the woods. In response to her defiance, the vengeful Hamleigh family attacks the earl's castle and jails him for treason. They then dispossess him and drive Aliena and her brother, Richard, out of the castle after William Hamleigh rapes her. Having been brought to the bottom of her fortunes, Aliena develops a talent for trade, which bit by bit restores her to the world of influence and property, although she is still without her land and title. Setbacks force her to repeat the building of her fortune, but she always rebounds to a level of substance and power. Given the constraints on women in the Middle Ages, Aliena could not have achieved what she did on her own, but in the novel she is clearly the prime mover in her ventures and she is directly or indirectly at the center of all the major events of the novel. Shut out from the world of power and inherited wealth and property, she makes her mark in the new area of trade and commerce, an area that was somewhat suspect to the medieval church, but is very familiar to modern readers. Aliena, as her name suggests, becomes an outsider in a landowning society and then succeeds in the parallel world of finance. Like Ellen, who had placed herself outside the reaches of church and state, Aliena finds a way to succeed and finally recover her birthright, through operating within the gray areas of religious and secular law which were open to a woman or other marginal members of society.

Philip Gynedd rivals Ellen and Aliena in terms of presence and importance in the novel, but his force and effectiveness is limited by his vow to live a retired and contemplative life. A talented Benedictine monk and prior of St. John's in the Forest, Philip first comes into prominence by demonstrating his managerial skills in making an unproductive priory a success. The increasingly complicated plot has Philip find the infant that Tom the Builder had abandoned in the forest. A man of equanimity and decency, Philip offers a positive role model of how people should behave. He faces the temptations of all the worldly vices as he rises and becomes more and more important in the world, but he maintains a clear sense of his purpose and a careful openness to the opportunities that life brings. Early in the novel, without knowing who she is, Philip helps Aliena make her first business deal as an act of charity. From then on, they create an important and powerful partnership, which threatens to engage Philip more and more with the world and move him further away from his spiritual foundations. He pursues his goal of serving God in his community through his work with Aliena and in political relations as a reluctant participant in the fighting for the crown of England. Through all of this worldly activity he remains true to his original vows, although the strength of those vows is tested in a number of ways. Philip's basic goodness remains as he changes other aspects of his view of life in response to the challenges he meets in his career.

William Hamleigh, the major villain in the story, remains consistent throughout. The suspense and tension surrounding him lie only in whether or not one or another of his schemes will succeed. He seems to get his way often enough to make him a constant threat, while his character and impulses are sufficiently despicable to encourage the reader to anticipate his suffering and defeat. His first appearance presents the range of characteristics that shape his behavior throughout the novel. He arrives in a rage at the site where Tom the Builder is working on his house, dismisses the workers, and refuses to pay them their due wages. The combination of arrogance, cruelty, and threatened violence that pervades his actions reveals his brutal and corrupt nature. When Tom opposes him and claims that, whatever the outcome of a fight, Tom will end up in heaven and the young lord in hell, William suddenly freezes and accedes, suggesting to Tom and to the reader that William is neurotic as well as brutal. William's fear of hell appears repeatedly, and the reader learns that he had been frightened as a child by stories of hell told by his mother. His neurotic side shades off into perversion as the reader learns later in the novel that William cannot experience sexual pleasure unless it is attended by cruelty and that much of his adult life is a warped and desperate nightmare. His hanging at the end of the novel seems inevitable from the beginning and only the turns of a complex plot might have delayed such a fate. His hanging fulfills the curse placed on his father by Ellen in the Prologue and parallels the hanging that opens the novel.

Plot Development

Not surprisingly in a novel about the building of a cathedral, the action is confined for the most part to the region around the cathedral town of Kingsbridge, but it advances and is complicated by occasional journeys, wanderings, and exiles of some of the characters. Within the region itself, the action is often set in motion by schemes to attack and defend one or another of the central properties around Kingsbridge. Because power and wealth in the Middle Ages derived from land, both secular and church-held, the conflicts in the novel focus on the local attempts by petty landowners and ambitious clerics to increase their property and influence. These conflicts are set within and are influenced by the larger historical framework of the factions warring for the crown of England. For every scheme and attack that is repulsed or defeated, another seems to rise in its place. The chaos of the conflicts among the aristocracy causes and is reflected in the difficult economic and social lives of the common people. The ebb and flow of these temporal events are cast into an ironic light by the elegant theological reasoning that warrants the building of cathedrals. The urge to reflect the majesty and power of God through the building of a cathedral expresses the driving force behind much of the good in the world of the novel and is contrasted with the personal and selfish drives of other characters, which exemplify what is wrong in that world. Through these two poles the novel presents a range of human values and virtues.

The pattern of wandering and settling begins early in the novel with Tom the Builder's search for permanent work. He has to leave the area around Kingsbridge and wanders throughout the shire until he finally finds a job at Earlscastle, the home of Earl Robert, Aliena, and Richard. But the work is short-lived when the Hamleighs attack the castle and take Earl Robert prisoner. Tom and his family move on to Kingsbridge, finding work only after Jack, Ellen's son, sets fire to the cathedral being built there. Once Tom is settled into working on the cathedral, he stays there until he dies. Ellen has to leave for a year after she is denounced by some of the monks, but she returns. After Tom's death, his eldest son, Alfred, is appointed cathedral builder; later in the novel Jack succeeds him. Thus the cathedral continues to be built, although it is threatened from time to time.

The relationship of Jack and Aliena mirrors the other wanderings in the novel. Jack leaves Kingsbridge when Aliena agrees to marry Alfred. Then she sets off on a journey to find Jack after Alfred denounces her upon the birth of a child who is clearly Jack's. Aliena's journey with her newborn child is long and heroic. As soon as she finds Jack, they decide that their calling lies with the cathedral and so they return to Kingsbridge. In all these developments within the family of Tom the Builder, the cathedral remains the constant even as the people face various challenges. The family members change and grow, but these changes shape the family and contribute to building the cathedral.

The steadfastness of the cathedral and the ecclesiastical and secular infrastructure that grows up around it is tested repeatedly by the ambitious and avaricious villains led by the unscrupulous priest Waleran Bigod and the Hamleighs. They create a constant stream of action and crisis in the novel as they plot to take over one or another of the properties and establishments built up around the Kingsbridge cathedral. Their efforts require that the other characters respond to the threat and defend themselves in order to preserve what they regard as their own, by right or by mission. As one attack is repulsed, the villains regroup to plan another, their constant and relentless effort making them a formidable enemy. The extended family rises to each of these challenges and contributes to the eventual defeat of the villains. But none of the family members accomplishes a heroic individual action. Rather, their collective courage and integrity prove too strong for the determined villains. The family becomes the hero of this saga by its constant vigilance and dedicated concern for its members. The genre of the saga showcases a cohesive and magnificent group of people whose shared values exemplify how both religious and secular communities can succeed in the world and in the eyes of God.

Thematic Issues

Perhaps the major theme in the novel is the conflict between using material wealth for spiritual and artistic ends and using it for personal power and pleasure. The importance of money is introduced early in the novel when it is noted that Tom the Builder had lost his job working on the previous cathedral because the master builder had mismanaged the money. The detail creates an awareness that the lofty purposes that inspire the building of cathedrals cannot carry the projects by themselves; cathedrals and all other human enterprises need careful and conscientious management. The monasteries, communities established to pursue the work of God in the world, turn out to need careful management as much as any other enterprise. The management of earldoms and knightly estates, as well as the financing of bids for thrones, also requires sound financial footing. The economic base derived from the hierarchic theological structure proves to be inadequate to withstand the stresses of political and social turmoil. This focus on the importance of economic interests asks the reader to consider the connections between emergent capitalism and land-based feudalism, and how these different systems treat human aspirations and occupations. Aliena's inventiveness raises the prospect of an economic alternative to landholding and suggests that the changes that led to the modern world were for the better.

In the novel both commercial and ecclesiastical endeavors offer lessons on the virtues of inventive and imaginative uses of resources. Philip Gynedd and Aliena's inventive use of resources proves profitable and productive for both, and their partnership suggests a compatibility between capitalism and medieval Christianity that is often denied in the theological pronouncements of the period. Aliena's improvements on the estates she holds in trust for Richard while he is off on a crusade suggest that the entrepreneurial spirit works for agricultural as well as mercantile systems. The novel argues that the apparent opposition between capitalism and spirituality may be overstated and misleading. Money comes to stand for power in the medieval world in the same way that it does in the modern world, and that equation confirms Follett's idea that all people in all ages respond to the same incentives and pursue similar values. Philip worries often about his engagement in worldly concerns, as well he should, given his vows as a monk. But the reader recognizes that Philip does not cross the materialistic line that would betray his religious vow. The reader is likely to celebrate the successful coexistence of money and spirituality in the novel.

The theme of the proper place of money extends to other characters whom the modern reader would recognize as middle class. Agnes's aspirations to a safe and comfortable home as well as the controversy that seems to follow Aliena's material success suggest the kinds of concerns about money that mark modern novels. The novel highlights the apparent opposition between material pursuits and the spiritual interests of cathedral builders such as Tom and the artists and inventors such as Jack and his father, Jack Cherbourg. The medieval world, without the explicit presence of money, could sustain the work of artists and inventors, but the impulse to succeed in material terms creates a conflict between the two realms, a conflict dramatized when Philip, pressed for money and desperate to meet a deadline, uses financial incentives to press Alfred to finish the cathedral, incentives that lead Alfred to cut corners in the building and set up the tragedy that occurs when the walls collapse during the dedication ceremony.

The novel raises interesting questions about the connection between belief and knowledge in the modern world. In the Middle Ages belief ranges from Ellen's curse in the Prologue to the deep spirituality that drives the building of cathedrals. Some of these beliefs might strike modern readers as superstitious until subsequent events in the novel give them some credence. The fates threatened in Ellen's curse do indeed come to pass. Jack's "Weeping Lady" icon, for whose occasional tears a rational explanation exists, is nevertheless the miracle that Philip needed to keep building the cathedral. The superstitions that prove to be true and the miracles that interact with economic and political forces ask modern readers to moderate their usual skepticism about miracles and superstitions as well as their absolute confidence in knowledge. The negotiations between belief and knowledge that work for the characters in the novel suggest ways for readers to settle conflicts between belief and knowledge in the modern world.

Another theme concerns the status of women both in the world of the novel and in modern society. This theme is introduced early when Tom and Agnes cannot understand why the marriage between Aliena and William has to be canceled because she does not want to marry him. It is inconceivable to them that she should have any say in the matter, a point of view that emphasizes the difference between the status of women in the Middle Ages and the late twentieth century. Aliena represents a catalogue of the issues that women have had to face in order to gain fair treatment in Western society. Similarly, William Hamleigh's attitudes and behavior reflect the extensive freedom that twelfth-century nobles enjoyed. Aliena's bold, aggressive actions define her as a heroine, which Jack acknowledges when he first sees her in action. Jack, by contrast, is the indirect and inventive victim who responds with cleverness rather than with aggression. He seeks companionship and artistic support rather than individual achievement and domination over others, thus offering an alternative to Hamleigh or Alfred.

The novel touches on the complexities of the psyche in its depiction of Hamleigh in terms that echo modern understanding of personality development. The reader recognizes that Hamleigh's behavior arises from a series of neurotic and eventually psychotic aspects of his personality: he is dependent upon his mother's opinion and confused in his sexual orientation and interests and unaware of his psychological handicaps. The presence of a thoroughly Freudian personality in this medieval setting amounts to another argument for the continuity of human urges and passions, an important element in Ken Follett's approach to his historical fiction.

A DANGEROUS FORTUNE

Ken Follett returns to the saga format with *A Dangerous Fortune*, focusing narrowly on the history of one family in one generation and on the place of money in modern society. The novel looks at the family banking fortunes that grew up in mid-nineteenth century England. These newly rich bankers and industrial entrepreneurs, whose fortunes were largely based on mercantile and industrial success, pressed society to accord them the same social power and distinction that had formerly accrued to the medieval aristocracy based on land. Indeed, Augusta Pilaster, the matriarch of the banking family at the center of this novel, makes acquiring a noble title the chief goal of her later life. Thus, Follett locates this saga in the period of the Industrial Revolution. In his usual way, he keeps his fiction close to actual historical fact and has based this story on the near collapse of the Barings Brothers bank, which invested too deeply in risky South American interests during the late nineteenth century.

For generations of readers who grew up on TV family sagas such as *Dallas*, some elements of *A Dangerous Fortune* should be familiar. The enormously rich family has an elaborate set of inner dynamics that drives the plot of the novel. The head of the Pilasters is also the head of the bank, thus making the family dynamics a controlling feature of the business world. As one of the two most powerful banks in a nation feeling the strength of a booming industrial and mercantile economy, the Pilaster bank stands as a symbol of an important age in English history, one that in some respects still shapes modern-day expectations in both England and the United States.

Point of View

The narrator of *A Dangerous Fortune* plunges the reader into a sudden and suspiciously violent action, which leads to a boy's mysterious death by drowning. How it will affect the story of the Pilaster fortune is unclear, but it raises questions for the reader and emphasizes his or her dependence on the narrator, who offers and withholds information. Follett uses an omniscient narrator, who knows all the actions and thoughts of all the characters and occasionally offers personal perspectives. Most of the information the reader receives comes from the perspectives of the various characters with the narrator filling in the details and events that are needed to tell the whole story. The narrator moves in and out of the characters' consciousnesses as needed. For instance, the Prologue ends with a conversation between Augusta Pilaster and Micky Miranda told from Augusta's point of view. Since she is the adult in the conversation, her observations about Miranda's strengths and determination indicate to the reader that these two people will be major players in the novel. The Prologue ends with the narrator reporting on Augusta's "wondering, with a distinct feeling of apprehension, how that handsome, knowing boy would use his power" (29). The reader has the benefit of Augusta's insight as well as the perception that she is attracted to Micky as well. These aspects of their first meeting shape the relationship between Micky and Augusta throughout the rest of the novel. Thus, the narrator uses point of view to guide the reader to the important and telling details of the story.

Character Development

In this saga the action arises from the developing and shifting relationships among the members of the Pilaster family and the other families whose fortunes intersect with it. The plot is driven by their complex family dynamics and control of the bank that bears their name. Both the family and the bank are determined in rigid and ritualized detail by the behavior of earlier generations. The stolid and steady traditions of the family work well in the banking business, although some of them are less well suited to a healthy family life. The family itself, characterized by its solid Methodist beliefs, represents the determined middle-class values and virtues that fared well in England during the last half of the nineteenth century.

The most engaging and positive character in the novel, the closest person to warranting the designation of hero, is Hugh Pilaster, a younger cousin of Edward Pilaster, who is the son of Augusta and Joseph Pilaster. Although present at the swimming hole on the day of the drowning, Hugh has no direct knowledge of the accident but finds it increasingly important during his adult life to trace what happened. On that day he hears that his father, Tobias Pilaster, who had previously taken his money out of the family bank, has committed suicide upon learning that his new business has failed. Hugh spends the rest of his life overcoming the shame of his father's failure and suicide. Those circumstances make him the poor cousin to be tolerated and condescended to at the bank and in the Pilaster home, where he stays after leaving school and coming to work at the bank. Hugh shows talent and interest in banking but is prevented for a long time from filling his proper role by Augusta Pilaster's machinations to ensure that her son, Edward, takes over the senior partnership at the bank. When the bank crashes as a result of Edward's mismanagement, Hugh is the person who holds the family together and enables it to survive the bankruptcy and prepare for the reestablishment of the Pilaster bank. Hugh's decency and sense of integrity allow him to avoid most of Augusta's plots and finally to overcome her power and influence in the family. Hugh emerges at the end as the head of the bank and the savior of the family.

Edward Pilaster leaves the pond at the beginning of the novel convinced that he is responsible for the drowning and indebted to his friend, Micky Miranda, for covering up for him. Edward's inability to think for himself and his affection for and dependence on Micky characterize his whole life. He has the same deference for and dependence on his mother, Augusta, and both people exploit his weak, superficial nature for their own ends. His mother has a twisted maternal affection for him while Micky only uses him, but both corrupt him in their own ways. In a Victorian family that has embraced the virtues of hard work and earnestness, Edward's capacity for pleasure and debauchery stands out in vivid contrast, and it takes all the power of his endlessly ambitious mother to keep him in places of importance. Edward's attachment to Micky seems neurotic from the first and then appears to be a latent homosexuality. Finally it is his pathetic emotional and sexual dependence on Micky that leads him to sacrifice the good of his family and the family business to Micky's interests.

Augusta Pilaster, Edward's mother and Hugh's aunt, married into the family in order to pursue her blinding ambition. Hugh's mother succinctly describes what anyone can expect of Augusta: "No matter what she has, she always wants more: more money, a more important job for her husband, a higher social position for herself. The reason she is so ambitious—for herself, for Joseph and for Edward—is that she still yearns for what Strang could have given her: the title, the ancestral home, the life of endless leisure, wealth without work" (202). Augusta's character never changes, but her power and presence diminish throughout the novel as she goes deeper and deeper into complicity with Micky. Augusta appears to be forbidding and determined, but she has enough perverse and corrupt inclinations to cloud her judgment and threaten her discipline. These weaknesses make her vulnerable in a world based on the assumption that only hard work and tight control over emotions can avoid disgrace and failure and promise material and social success. Releasing her passion for Micky at the very end almost completes her degradation and fall from prominence and power. Her ability to survive that final crisis and live on in isolation and reduced circumstances is a measure of her iron, but twisted, will. Augusta offers a dangerous and imposing threat to all that is good. Her unbounded scheming and amoral pursuit of her own ends comes to stand for the worst in society, and the relentless energy that she brings to bear in undermining all that the reader perceives to be good seems like an inversion of the energy and steadfastness that Victorians, and Pilasters specifically, applied to fuel the rise of the British economy. Her unchecked ambition stands as a metaphor for what can go wrong in society when its very impressive ordering forces take a wrong turn.

Micky Miranda, the other main character at the pond, is the image of an almost perfect Machiavellian. He thirsts for power and is willing to use money, sex, friendship, and social standing to achieve it. His actions in and responses to his world are chilling. Motivated partly by fear of his father's wrath and hatred of his brother, Micky commits four murders and ruins many lives. His fear and resentment of his father and brother reveal his weaknesses, so the reader never develops any respect or admiration for him. Driven by these negative and neurotic feelings, he never has a chance of keeping up with the discipline and commitment of the hard-working Victorians he competes with. Cordova, the fictional South American country he comes from, is brutal and unforgiving, in stark contrast to the commercial and social world of London, which is extremely civilized and tolerant. Micky, like Shakespeare's villain Iago in *Othello*, is a figure who introduces corruption and deceit into the lives of others in order to serve his own ends and to express his own envy.

The other major character introduced in the Prologue is Maisie Robinson, who is, like Hugh, a positive and balanced figure. She brings a directness in her approach to life and a joy in living that are absent from much of the Victorian society depicted in the novel. Maisie's experiences in life offer a parallel to those of the Pilaster family, a parallel especially noticeable because her path was set by the first Pilaster bankruptcy, the failure of Tobias's business. Maisie's father epitomizes the ideal of hard work and dedication that is the cornerstone of Victorian values, and his helplessness when the business goes under gives the lie to the promise that hard work and clean living will be rewarded. Without a job and with his wife in poor health, Maisie's father has no options and no hope. In a grim replay of the Hansel and Gretel story, Maisie and her brother leave home because there is no food for them. Dan, Maisie's brother, stows away on a ship bound for America, and Maisie finds her way to working with a traveling circus. Maisie reenters the world of the Pilasters when she encounters the young Hugh, Edward, and Micky out on the town while she is providing easy company for Solly Greenbourne, whom Hugh and the others knew at Wingfield School. Maisie and Hugh fall in love, but after they are discovered together in the Pilaster home, Augusta engineers their separation and sends Hugh packing to America. Maisie marries Solly and becomes a very influential and popular hostess in London, eclipsing people like Augusta in importance and influence through her friendship with the Prince of Wales. Her friend April introduces Maisie at one point as the "woman who did all we dream of" (352), and her rise from rags to riches approximates all that is found in most tales of that sort, with the exception that she has not found the happiness that she would have had with Hugh. Referring to the same rise, Augusta describes her as "the greatest parvenu of them all" (489).

Maisie has a social conscience, and, along with Rachel Bodwin, Micky Miranda's ex-wife, she founds and operates a home for unwed mothers and battered women in London. The work gives her a cause of her own, a position from which to challenge the hypocrisy of Victorian society, and a focus for her passionate beliefs and energy. The success of the home parallels the development of the bank, except that her institution is dedicated to community service while the bank is based upon a thoroughgoing nineteenth-century individualism. Maisie voices the values and concerns that have only begun to surface in Victorian society, but which come to be a central aspect of the public debate about work and profit found in the novels of Charles Dickens. Her fortunes rise and fall throughout the novel, but they are always close to the main action of the bank and the Pilaster family. When all the turns of the plot have played out, Maisie emerges as the partner with Hugh in the founding of the next stage of the Pilaster family and fortune.

Plot Development

The shifting perspectives through which the opening event of the Prologue is narrated leave the reader with a sense of mystery about what happened at the pond and suggest that the course of the novel will be shaped by that event. The very end of the novel returns to the scene of the drowning and seems to confirm that the events of that day and subsequently arose from mysterious and dangerous origins: "It was almost as if something evil had come up out of the deep water that day in 1866 and entered their lives, bringing all the dark passions that had blighted their lives, hatred and greed and selfishness and cruelty; fomenting deceit, bankruptcy, disease and murder" (568). The reader, however, recognizes that the events in the novel and the motives that drive the people account for the suffering and misery. The sense of complexity and ambiguity about motives adds the feeling that aspects of this saga are tragic. The "fortune" of the title refers, then, both to the money that sits at the center of the bank and to the sense that characters are being manipulated by forces much larger and more irresistible than their own desires.

The Prologue introduces two strands of the story, the "fortunes" of the Pilaster family proper and its bank and the "fortunes" of Maisie and Dan Robinson, who rise from poverty and homelessness to positions of power and influence. The two strands offer a variety of perspectives on the social, economic, and psychological values of English society in the last half of the nineteenth century.

Tragedies often depict the fall of a character who has reached a position of power and importance. This saga does not meet the strict criteria for tragedy, but a number of its characters' fortunes rise and fall. At the opening of the novel, both Augusta Pilaster and Micky Miranda are doing well and are on the rise. Augusta works, albeit deceitfully and ruthlessly, to have her husband become the senior partner at the bank and eventually a titled lord. Micky arranges for arms shipments to his father, is appointed to a diplomatic post he covets, and works finally to provide the backing for his father's overthrow of the legitimate government in Cordova and ultimately for Micky's own ascendancy to power there. Augusta's and Micky's plans and schemes keep working until the web of deceit and violence becomes so complex that it finally works against itself and brings down the Pilaster bank. The fortunes of Hugh and Maisie, who represent noble and honest impulses and behavior and are often the objects of Micky's and Augusta's scheming, fall as the villains rise, and finally rise as the villains fall. At the opening of the novel both Hugh and Maisie face events that destroy their chances for happiness and success. The action follows their alternating disappointments and successes. The rise and fall of the fortunes of these four major characters constitutes the pattern of action in the novel. The family dynamics provide the pace and the shape of that action.

The novel covers the passing of one generation. The action is divided chronologically into months by chapter. Each month represents a victory of the persistence of the family and also marks the deadline for each test of the family integrity. Although the aged uncle Seth is alive and in control at the opening, he does not play a central role; most of the action centers around Augusta's efforts to secure a position and title for her husband and eventually for her son. The suspense and tension arise from the struggles between the good and evil characters to control the money and the family and the ever present possibility that Augusta and Micky, who are willing to do evil to attain their ends, might succeed. A family and an institution with extraordinary traditions and values has strengths and resources, but the assault on those strengths from within threatens the order within the family and the world outside it. Readers can see the connections between the fortunes of the fictional family and their own experiences with success and disappointment in the world.

Thematic Issues

The major theme of *A Dangerous Fortune*, referred to in the title, is the importance of money to society and to individuals. The connection between money and values is emphasized by a fiction that focuses on the family and the bank as coextensive operations. When the family is notable primarily for their financial holdings, then human values and motives come into conflict with successful business practices. The exuberant capitalist economy of the late nineteenth century has clearly replaced the land-based economy and appropriated the social and political structures that had evolved around it. The most dramatic view of this process comes in the bitter words of the socially scheming Augusta as she comments on the guests at Hugh's sister's wedding: " 'London society has degenerated completely,' Augusta said to Colonel Mudeford. . . . 'Breeding counts for nothing anymore,' she went on. 'Jews are admitted everywhere.' . . . 'I was the first countess of Whitehaven, but the Pilasters were a distinguished family for a century before being honored with a title; whereas today a man whose father was a navvy can get a peerage simply because he made a fortune selling sausages' " (488). Augusta's failure to recognize her own social climbing in her description of the degeneration of London society exemplifies a rising middle class that sees itself already at home with those above it and at a distance from those below it. Extraordinary fortunes such as the Pilaster money threaten the established social order because economic power means more than social tradition in an increasingly trade-oriented society such as nineteenth-century England.

The novel raises the question of whether money is indeed the defining criterion of life. The crimes that pervade the novel and threaten the continuation of the family were committed for the sake of money and power. Decency and honesty, which were formerly the hallmarks of civilized behavior, are undercut here. Indeed, Maisie and Hugh, who represent traditional values, find themselves isolated and marginalized for failing

to make financial gain their primary goal. Money makes a very big difference in the lives depicted in the novel, but the novel asks the reader
to affirm the moral distinctions and terms that ought to limit money as
a motive for action. The novel offers examples of the destructive consequences of substituting money for higher values. Hugh's wife, Nora,
represents a case of displaced values when she literally, but not explicitly, trades sex for gifts, making the investment of her affection and her
person contingent on a payment of material goods. Maisie flings a similar
charge at Augusta by suggesting that married women of the upper classes sell their favors every bit as much as do single, working-class girls.

The novel certainly suggests that individual human dignity depends
more on respect than on money: Maisie's defiant behavior from the beginning makes that point. But her dramatic individualism is made more
precise in her campaign for fair and decent treatment of women, which
is another major theme in the novel. The Pilaster wives are powerful
only as they operate indirectly through the Pilaster men. Maisie operates
as an independent woman and supports the rights of women. Her letter
to the *Times* cites as an example of woman's equality with, and perhaps
superiority to, men an unmarried mother at her shelter and asks the
reader to sympathize with the woman's position and disavow the patriarchal view expressed by the other letter writers. Maisie's own life and
career represent both the struggles women faced in Victorian society,
where they had very few legal rights, and the triumphs that accrue to
determined and talented women. Maisie joins the long list of Follett heroines who share the spotlight with, and sometimes upstage, the male
heroes in his novels. Follett, noted for his strong and engaging women,
creates in Maisie another successful woman whose portrayal invites the
reader to affirm the values she represents. Augusta, for all her malevo-
lence and despicable behavior, is a strong woman, and most of the family
treat her as if she were the center of family power. Follett regards her
as one of his most successful female characters (Interview, 22 May 1995).
Although few readers will identify with or admire Augusta, she commands respect for her iron will and determination. Despite her deplorable motives, her success at attaining power within a hostile world
establishes her as a major character. She and Maisie both acquire power
and influence; the novel is concerned with the differences in their motives and methods.

The novel also suggests that money levels the social and political playing fields, creating inroads into society's entrenched groups, a theme that
is almost an ironic corollary of Augusta's complaint about the degener-

acy of social orders. Money makes it possible for talented and hard-working people such as Ben Greenbourne and Hugh Pilaster to measure their successes and claim their rewards. Money can promote tolerance and make possible equal treatment of people, as at the women's shelter, which is threatened as soon as the bank fails. These openings within a society closed by class consciousness and sexism amount to an important breakthrough. Money offers a way to change some very basic values in the world of the novel. Dan Robinson discovers that social change and justice for deprived groups can be effected if one operates from a sound financial base. With independent financial resources, he finally moves on to a seat in Parliament as a way to bring about the social changes in which he believes.

Literary Devices

A Dangerous Fortune uses figures of speech in much the same way other Follett novels do. Imaginative similes bring color to the story: Augusta tries to feign pleasantness "like a dragon trying to purr" (110), and Tonio Silva's attitude toward Micky Miranda is "like a puppy with a cruel master" (143). The allusions to Kingsbridge, the site of the cathedral in *The Pillars of the Earth,* and the repeated appearances of a made-up pornographic novel, *The Duchess of Sodom,* may be playful: Follett's attempt at a little in-joke with his regular readers. Micky finds a copy of *The Duchess of Sodom* in Tonio's room, Maisie finds a copy as she rummages around Hugh's room, and Augusta finds a copy in Joseph's chest of drawers when she is searching for valuables. Although the book is mentioned only in passing, the repetition suggests Follett's interest in Victorians' hidden taste for pornography. This suggests the inadequacy of Victorian education about sexual matters and reflects a now widely accepted view that Victorians were hypocrites in regard to sexuality. Follett also glances at the matter of Victorian pornography in *The Man from St. Petersburg.*

A MARXIST APPROACH TO *THE PILLARS OF THE EARTH* AND *A DANGEROUS FORTUNE*

Marxist literary criticism focuses on the social, political, and economic forces that shape literary texts. It articulates the values and pressures in society that influence the creation of the text. In particular, a Marxist literary critic pays special attention to the interactions of class and ideology in a text. Such a critic of *The Pillars of the Earth* might examine the economic forces at work in the novel. A Marxist reading would analyze character and plot in terms of the early capitalistic practices of the time. The novel focuses on a moment in English history when feudalism is under pressure, from leaders centralizing their political power, to create a nation-state based on a capitalist economy. Material concerns generate the conflicts and the suspense in the novel and so invite a Marxist critical analysis. Aliena's talent for making money and turning a profit at occupations that had previously been merely nonprofit pursuits enables her to resist the combined forces of an aristocratic family and a corrupted church hierarchy. The events surrounding the lives of Tom the Builder and his family also invite a Marxist reading. Tom represents the medieval working-class peasant. He is actually an artisan and so an economic step above a peasant, but that distinction only highlights the importance of the means of production. In a traditional agricultural economy the workers are interchangeable in the eyes of the consumers of that labor, in this case the lords. Tom the Builder and other artisans complicate the economic relationships in that economy because they possess information and expertise and trade them for money, power, and personal satisfaction. Thus, the novel introduces major elements of the modern world into its medieval setting. Although the church may have intended cathedrals as monuments to the status quo and reminders of heavenly aspirations, the actual process of building them introduces the forces that will drive modern political economies. A Marxist reading of the novel would point out the degree to which the shift in material values changes the society and the people in the novel. The story of the families central to *The Pillars of Wisdom* depicts the historical and material forces that changed the medieval world and the origins of the struggle between the classes that would lead to modern society.

Since *A Dangerous Fortune* focuses on a nineteenth-century banking family, a casual reader might think that a Marxist reading of the novel would merely point out the corrosive effects of capitalism and its oppression of working people; and indeed the antipathy between the bankers and Dan Robinson's labor organizing might enforce that perception. But *A Dangerous Fortune* might be more interesting to a Marxist critic in terms of the relations among the bankers in the novel than in terms of its depictions of class conflict. The shifts in power and the responsibilities for the rise and fall of the bank's fortunes show a range of approaches toward money, value, and power and their connections with banking practices. Augusta Pilaster drives the bank into ruin because she does not understand the connection between money and how money is produced and used to generate further wealth. She sees only the connection between money and social power. Hugh Pilaster and Maisie Robinson understand the proper uses of money and so are able to convert desire and vision into sound realities by keeping money closely tied to its appropriate functions. In another aspect of a material analysis of culture and society, Hugh succeeds through skill and so competes with the already wealthy by using money better than they can. The importance of the means of production, even among bankers, emphasizes the Marxist point about how societies need to keep contributions to wealth and rewards for those contributions in balance in order to foster healthy change and development. Hugh crosses class lines in his pursuit of Maggie Robinson, and their union at the end reflects the importance of solidarity among workers in the struggle for material wealth and power in Western societies.

The other major element in the plot, the machinations of Micky Miranda, can also be given a Marxist analysis. Micky's family in Cordova schemes to wrest control of the country and its wealth by force under the guise of a people's revolution. The Marxist critic would point to the need to recognize false prophets. The Pilaster bank's failure to see the weakness of investing in Cordova and Augusta's willingness to go along with what was in effect blackmail for Micky's silence undercut the bank's soundness and bring it to destruction. That a few members of an elite could ruin a bank's fortune does indeed suggest to the Marxist the failure of capitalism. Follett himself might not be a Marxist, but a Marxist analysis of his books reveals aspects of society and the forces that drive present-day economies, revelations that should prod a reader to examine modern economic conditions as instances of proper or inappropriate handling of the material dynamics of society and culture.

Night over Water
(1991) and
A Place Called Freedom
(1995)

In both *Night over Water* and *A Place Called Freedom* the characters head for America, but the function of America in the two novels differs greatly. In *Night* America is most important as a destination—of the plane, whose transatlantic journey provides the engaging and thrilling action of the novel, and of the passengers and crew, whose experiences during the flight help them to realize important aspirations or resolve personal conflicts. In *Place* eighteenth-century America is a setting—the site of the final stage of the extended escape attempt and the chase that appears so often in Follett's novels. As such, it is an example of Follett's frequent use of historically and geographically remote locales. In addition, colonial America is an explicit symbol of the values and interests at the center of the novel, thus serving as a plot device and theme.

NIGHT OVER WATER

Night over Water continues Ken Follett's interest in placing his novels in historical settings that offer a sense of importance as well as excitement. The action takes place on the eve of World War II as the Pan American Airways super clipper, an airliner built specifically for transatlantic flights and designed to keep passengers in a state of total luxury, makes its last peacetime flight. War hovers over the novel, and, as in other novels, Follett takes advantage of this historically compelling moment.

The plane itself becomes a character in the novel and shapes the action. The first sentence makes the extravagant claim that it was "the most romantic plane ever made" (3), and it is described as "enormous, majestic, unbelievably powerful, an airborne palace" (4-5). One extraordinary aspect of the plane is its tendency to level distinctions between social classes. People whose paths would ordinarily not cross find themselves in close proximity and often in conversation. The routine of flight requirements and the extraordinary moments of crisis throw different people into a common situation and insist that they work together and depend upon one another. Thus, as the plane travels from the solidly hierarchic societies of Europe to the more egalitarian America, the trip over the Atlantic requires the erasing of class distinctions. Most of the action takes place within the plane on this twenty-seven-hour flight. Thus it follows mystery precedents such as Agatha Christie's *Murder on the Orient Express*, in which the entire action from crime to investigation to solution takes place on a train journey. In other mysteries and thrillers, country houses, remote castles, even ocean liners provide the confining location that brings people together for the duration of the action. An airplane on an overnight journey, however, might be the most confining setting yet, in terms of both time and place. Follett follows the mystery and thriller precedent by including a chase element, although the chase occurs in stages and the frenetic final stages are augmented by people who board the plane after it has landed.

The plane can be compared to an oceangoing luxury liner. The novel introduces the reader to a roster of characters who play out their concerns and conflicts during the flight, much like a special kind of work called "a ship of fools," after the title of the 1494 poem *Das Narrenschiff* by Sebastian Brandt, in which people on a ship represent human follies and vices. This format has been imitated a number of times, the most familiar to modern readers being Katherine Anne Porter's *Ship of Fools* (1962), which is set on an ocean liner headed for America in the 1930s. Like an allegory, in this kind of story each character represents one aspect of the human condition. Unlike the original poem and Porter's novel, which present a pessimistic and satiric view of human nature, Follett's view is much more optimistic. His characters are three-dimensional, rather than the two-dimensional characters of an allegory. The novel does, however, use the confined setting to dramatize conflicts in ways that would be impossible in other settings.

This novel is also a historical romance in that it emphases the feelings and reactions of the women. At regular intervals, the primary focus of the action is on whether or not one heroine or another should give her heart and/or her person to the man of the moment. Follett regularly presents strong female characters who play important, sometimes crucial, roles in the action, but the suspense is generated by public action while these heroines are engaged in making up their minds about love, the central drama of romance novels. Some of the other qualities of the men and women involved in these quandaries approximate the conventions of romance novels. Mervyn Lovesey resembles the typical romance hero, who is usually older than the woman and often strong and domineering (and only sensitive when the right woman finds out how to touch his sensitive soul) or, like Mark Alder, Mervyn's competitor for the love of Diana Lovesey, is sensitive and caring if outwardly retiring. Diana Lovesey is the quintessential romance heroine, who follows her heart at every turn. Harry Marks and Margaret Oxenford are a young couple who begin the journey with clearly defined values and objectives and are changed thoroughly by the love they discover on the journey. All the men and women engaged in these romances are unusually ready and eager for sensual experiences even if each of them is taken by surprise every time passion overwhelms his or her previous resistance.

Point of View

In a novel that emphasizes character, point of view takes on added importance. Because the narrator explains the prominence of the plane in aviation history and in the choices of wealthy and socially privileged people, the reader immediately has a sense of what a milestone this flight is. Most of the novel follows the pattern that is familiar in Follett novels: an omniscient narrator conveys the action, but most of the story is told through the consciousness of the characters. For the most part, each chapter following Part 1 is told from the perspective of one character. At times a chapter offers the perspectives of two characters who are at that moment deeply engaged with each other. This shift in perspective dramatizes the ebb and flow of emotion and commitment between them and gives the reader a sense of the excitement and rush of emotion going on in the characters' minds and hearts.

Because Part 1 establishes the plot lines that will drive the action of the novel and keep the reader engaged in the mystery and suspense, it has more shifts in point of view than any of the other sections. Each of the first five chapters introduces a set of characters who will play a major role in the novel, and the point of view shifts among them. Eddie Deakin, the flight engineer on whom the details of the kidnapping plot center, appears in all five chapters. The simultaneous points of view reflect the fact that their lives will be affected by what is happening to Eddie, since he is being asked to sabotage the plane at some point in the flight. The shifting points of view enable the reader to enter into the development of the novel as well as into the minds of the people who will be at the center of the action.

Through the perspective of Eddie Deakin, Follett gives the reader a feeling for the technological marvel of the Pan American Airways super clipper. In carrying out his duties as flight engineer, Eddie introduces the reader to the marvels of the new plane, the complex and intricate planning that went into building it, and the precise logistics necessary to complete the transatlantic journey. If the average bystander is impressed with the size and power of the plane, Eddie's view creates a sense of the delicacy and fragility of operating it. The clipper might be as large and capacious as an ocean liner, but the insider's point of view alerts the reader to how much care is needed to keep it flying.

An episode that shows the effective use of point of view is Margaret Oxenford's adventure in blacked-out London in Part 1. Lost at night, she wanders through the streets in absolute darkness: "She crossed the road and found the opposite pavement without falling over it. That encouraged her and she walked on more confidently. Suddenly something smacked into her face with agonizing violence. She cried out in pain and sudden fear. For a moment she was in a blind panic and wanted to turn and run" (32). The description continues for another hundred or so words before she discovers that she has been "attacked by a pillar-box." The reader experiences this action with Margaret and gains a sense of what it means to be so suddenly and painfully surprised. Thus, point of view is effective in engaging the reader in the story as well as in the character's development.

The novel also uses overlapping points of view to convey insights and information about characters. Chapter 3 introduces Harry Marks, but it also offers a long observation Harry makes to himself about Margaret Oxenford. This passage provides the reader with useful insights into her character and what will become Harry's extraordinary interest in her. Having just seen Margaret's perspective in the second and third chapters, the reader can compare it to Harry's view of her.

Character Development

Aristotle's *Poetics* suggests that the effectiveness of a tragedy arises in part from a unified sense of time, place, and action, and his Renaissance followers developed these criteria into a rigid set of expectations about plays and other works. By even by those very strict measures, *Night* works within a strict and demanding discipline. Its action is remarkable because of its tight and intense development of character and plot, but the overwhelming energy of the novel lies in its characterization. The confined setting heightens the emphasis on characterization. The characters remain present and involved from the beginning to the end. They are never "off stage" as in other novels in which characters go off on their own for a while and then exhibit a change in perspective or attitude upon returning. Follett succeeds in creating three-dimensional characters who grow up, mature, expand their horizons, or rethink their values and priorities. They make sacrifices and commitments as well as discoveries about themselves and about people they thought they knew well. What creates the special interest for the reader and the special challenge for the writer is that all of these changes happen within the space of just over a day and within the confines of the airplane.

The main characters in *Night* pair up quickly. The one central character without a partner on the flight, Eddie Deakin, is reunited with his wife at the end, a pairing that reflects the romance quality of the novel. Margaret Oxenford, the young aristocrat, joins with Harry Marks, a jewel thief, and they set off at the end for a new life in Canada. Diana Lovesey exchanges her boring, insensitive husband for Mark Alder, a comedy show writer and radio station owner in California, and they begin a new life in America. Mervyn Lovesey, Diana's husband, pursues her and on the way meets Nancy Lenehan, an American businesswoman rushing back to America to save her control of her business. Mervyn and Nancy are thrown together by circumstance, but they become lovers on the journey and decide to live happily ever after in England.

Eddie Deakin seems at first glance to hold little promise as an engaging character, except for his central position as the agent of a plot to seize a passenger on the plane. He also seems a little out of place as a major character on this flight because his working-class background and interest in the mechanics of planes make him very different from the other people on the plane. But Eddie's character is developed first in terms of his integrity regarding machines and his duty and then regarding his response to the news that some thugs have kidnapped his wife and will rape and kill her if he fails to follow their instructions. Before getting the call from the thugs, Eddie appears as an expert at his job and committed to it because of his fascination with the machinery. His character flows directly from his interest and expertise. He loves his work and he loves his wife, and he experiences conflict because his job takes him away from his wife more than she wants it to. Eddie seems drawn to the work because of the excitement of the new technology, but he plans eventually to find a job closer to home. He comes across to the reader as decent and devoted, an average man trying to do his job and fulfill his talents and interests. He is someone the reader can trust.

Eddie makes a clear decision to do whatever he has to do to get his kidnapped wife back, although he expresses his anger to all the thugs. The narrator compares him to a kettle ready to boil and to a volcano; that sense of his mounting rage creates some of the tension in the novel. If Eddie cannot contain his rage, then the flight may be doomed; certainly his wife will be. The reader develops an admiration for Eddie's ability to maintain his control and perform the elaborate maneuvers necessary to bring the plane down where the thugs have specified. Although initially described as a "simple man," Eddie shows an increasingly sophisticated ability to negotiate the complicated choices that he faces throughout the flight. His values are clear, and he recognizes the consequences of his actions; this ability to keep all these demands in order makes him a hero even though he accommodates the thugs. At the end, he is quick to respond to his wife's hope that he can stop flying, and so they end up settling happily in America. Eddie suggests what an honest, hardworking, intelligent American can do when called upon. He stands as one of the points of strength in the novel.

Margaret Oxenford plays a central role because she engages many of the thematic concerns of the novel. She is, perhaps, the character who makes the greatest change, since she starts out as almost a helpless child under the control of her parents but becomes an independent woman who has made a deep commitment to a man and to a new life in a new country. The reader meets Margaret as she grows restive under the dominance of her father, a Nazi sympathizer, and her passive mother. Her father's political history forces the family to leave England to stay with the mother's family in Connecticut. Margaret wants to stay in England and fight in the war; she runs away from home in an attempt to assert her independence. The miserable failure of her attempt is a measure of just how unready she is to live independently no matter how much she wants to develop a separate identity from that of her parents. Her father cruelly spells out for her just how dependent she is and how unprepared to do anything on her own. During the plane flight Margaret comes to understand the meaning of acting on political convictions and takes some initial steps to establish her own relationships with people involved in current social and political movements. Her more mature approach to public action suggests the degree to which she has changed, although her continuing failure to grant her father any understanding suggests that she has some more maturing to do. She also makes a commitment to Harry Marks that extends beyond the very real delight she takes in the covert sexual relationship they strike up on the voyage. Her interest in Harry indicates an end to her mourning for her first love, a young idealist who had been killed two years earlier in the Spanish Civil War. Her commitment to Harry rises above the youthful idealism and childish resentment that seemed to motivate her earlier actions in the novel.

Along with her brother, Percy, Margaret represents hope for the continuation of aristocratic traditions. Although neither Margaret nor Percy has had a good education, and despite their upbringing by the founder of the British Union of Fascists and the author of a vicious racist tract, they both stand up for humane and civilized values and offer a brave and vigorous defense of the Jewish scientist whose capture is the aim of the thugs pressuring Eddie Deakin. Margaret's and Percy's entry into enlightened political understanding is all the more remarkable because their older sister, Elizabeth, has already left the family to follow her dreams to what she sees as the glories of Nazi Germany. Margaret's development from an immature idealist to a person willing to act on her convictions in practical and effective ways marks an important change in her character.

Margaret's father, Lord Oxenford, deteriorates during the flight from a stuffy, nasty racist and overbearing parent and husband to an obnoxious boor held in wide contempt by most of the passengers. The world of the plane becomes a place where titles and money mean very little. The reader's increasing impatience with Lord Oxenford's attitudes and behavior creates sympathy for Margaret and enthusiasm for her steps toward independence. The plane also carries an aristocrat whose behavior is in distinct opposition to Lord Oxenford's. Baron Gabon accompanies Carl Hartmann, the Jewish physicist on the run from the Nazis, as an act of generosity. He uses his power and influence as an aristocrat to help Jews escape Nazism and so offers a dramatic example of how aristocrats can fulfill the responsibilities of their rank in times of controversy and public travail.

Harry Marks, Margaret's lover, makes a palpable change during the flight. When the reader, and Margaret, first meet Harry, he has been arrested for stealing some jewels, a charge that he avoids through the kind of fast talking and easy character impersonation that have enabled him to get close to expensive jewelry in the first place. The reader finds out that he comes from a poor background and has used his wit and intelligence to develop the manners and habits of the aristocracy and so manage the jewel robberies that support his way of life. Harry is an expert on jewelry and good at jewel theft. He is interested in Margaret at their first meeting, but that interest seems limited to a vague sexual attraction. When they meet again on the clipper and have seats in the same compartment, they form a deeper friendship, and his attraction toward her increases. At the same time, it becomes clear that he faces a serious conflict because her mother's jewels, especially a valuable necklace called the Delhi Suite, could set him up for life once he reaches America. Harry suffers the conflict of love and lucre; he has to make a choice between Margaret and the $100,000 her mother's jewels could bring him.

Harry's change during the novel is remarkable. At the beginning he has no discernible goals except his own self-interest, and he seems to have no affection for anyone or loyalty to anything. During the course of the flight he learns about the importance of public and private values and the difference affection for and commitment to another person can make. Harry's debates with himself about the money versus a life with Margaret run the gamut of moral reasoning, beginning with purely selfish concerns and ending with a sense of both higher priorities and the value of devotion to another. In the course of these debates he even contemplates corrupting Margaret to complicity in the theft of her mother's jewels, so the reader understands how far Harry has come when he makes the decision to do the right thing. He is rewarded for his decision to go for love by the convenient plot device of stumbling on the $100,000 Tom Luther has brought on board to pay the thugs. Thus, at the end of the novel Harry is a new man, has won the girl of his dreams, and has enough money to live the kind of life in Canada he has always wanted. Readers sympathetic with his progress and who have accepted the transforming power of this night over water will applaud his good fortune.

Diana Lovesey and Mark Alder, the other runaways on the clipper, board the plane full of the thrill and expectation that a new romantic adventure can bring. Diana is a pretty, sensitive woman who has been caught for five years in a marriage with her dull and controlling husband, Mervyn. Her initial and subsequent meetings with Mark manifest how bored and desperate she is. Mark first speaks to her as she is escaping from a dinner dance attended by her husband's drunken associates and their wives. Mark is bright and interested in her and a big contrast to the unappetizing men at the dance. As her dissatisfaction with her marriage increases, she sees Mark again and they begin an affair that lasts through the summer. When Mark tells her he must return to America because of the impending war and asks her to come with him, she agrees. Then she decides against leaving, but Mark entices her back to her original decision. Another boring evening of Mervyn taking her for granted strengthens her resolve, and she leaves the next day. This lack of resolution characterizes Diana throughout the novel. Once on the plane, she regrets her decision, as Mark seems to ignore her while talking to an old friend. She argues with him about his behavior and they resolve their differences. Diana's superficial approach to her impending life change is conveyed by her angry thoughts about Mark for ignoring her.

During the course of the flight Diana continues to vacillate, but she is provoked to those moments of doubt by the arrival before takeoff of her husband, who has pursued her. Her final emergence as an independent person with a deep and respectable commitment to Mark is a direct response to Mervyn. Mervyn's arrival both flatters and worries Diana, and she has moments of hesitation and doubt when he first bullies her, demanding that she return and insisting that she cannot succeed on her own, and then confesses the error of his ways and pleads with her to return. The reader can see that her doubts arise more from old habits and insecurities than from any lingering affection for Mervyn. But Mark cannot be sure, and so Mervyn's presence creates a strain on their relationship, which, in turn, generates more moments of doubt and apprehension. Diana's fluctuating emotions create suspense about her development as a person and the success of her romantic adventure. Finally, she makes up her mind to leave Mervyn and forces him to face the real motives for his willingness to let her go. This moment marks her arrival as an independent person ready for the future, commitment to Mark, and likely success in California.

Mervyn Lovesey, a character who seems at first stolid and dull, becomes a dashing and heroic figure during the course of the novel. He seems simply focused and determined in his mission to retrieve his wife, but the other aspects of his personality come forward as he responds to the company of Nancy Lenehan and the difficulties he has to surmount to get what he wants. What Mervyn wants changes as the journey proceeds. The reader learns that his first wife left him in much the same way that Diana did. That experience, plus his controlling nature, appear to be his motives for pursuing Diana. At the end of the journey Mervyn is almost as brusque and direct in his dealings with people as he was in the beginning, and he is not much more ready to negotiate with Nancy, but he is more willing to express his love and interest in someone else and he seems to look forward to happiness with Nancy. Mervyn, who appeared to be ready to live his life in a rut at the beginning of the novel, steps up and outwits the thugs when they threaten to abduct Diana along with Carl Hartmann. Mervyn does not fight off the thugs on his own, but his quick thinking and brave confrontation defeat them and save the kidnap victims. Mervyn rises to the challenges of love and danger and ends the novel as a reluctant, somewhat gruff hero. He finds love and the prospect of happiness on the journey because of or in spite of his businesslike approach to life. The qualities that drove Diana into the arms of the creative and sensitive Mark make a positive impression on Nancy.

Mervyn's strength and forthrightness attract Nancy Lenehan because she is surrounded by deceit and double-dealing. She is effective and clearheaded in business, but her success has been undercut by a company structure that protects her brother's weak business sense and his nasty personal vendetta against her. Her motives for working so hard for the company are shown to be misplaced as the details of her father's intentions become clear. Nancy learns a lot about her business relationships during the flight, confirms her sense of herself as a tough and astute businesswoman, and discovers that she can continue her success in business and find personal happiness.

The narrator's observation that Nancy has started to gain weight at forty suggests the sense of deterioration that stimulates her journey across the Atlantic. She has to hurry to catch the plane because she has discovered that her brother is double-crossing her on a business deal. She works so hard to fight her brother for control of the company because she feels that she owes it to the memory of her father, who had worked so hard to build the business, but she finds out from a crony of his that he had engineered the conflicts with her brother so that the stronger person would end up in control of the company. That revelation appears to leave Nancy with the choice between life as a cutthroat in the harsh world of business and following her natural, altruistic instincts for nurturing, as seen in her treatment of Margaret Oxenford. Nancy's triumph at the end is that she not only beats her brother at the business deal but also finds a way to pursue her business interests with integrity and commit herself to a relationship with Mervyn Lovesey. Nancy's journey across the Atlantic resolves her conflict and provides a chance for the personal happiness that she has so long denied herself.

Three minor characters contribute to the plot development or the thematic concerns. Tom Luther, the American in the wool business who is on board to advance the kidnap plot, sets in motion the threat that hangs over the entire flight. But he does not develop as a character. He remains the same nervous conspirator he was when he enters the novel. He is revealed at the end to be a conspirator for a different cause from the one that Eddie Deakin and the reader at first supposed. His remarks identify him as an anti-Semite and an anti-Communist so strong in his hatred that he finds association with a Mafia chief an acceptable way of doing business. His ties with Nazism, revealed at the end, merely extend the reader's understanding of the kind of person he is. The ambiguity about whom Tom serves parallels the story line of the other thugs and suggests that Nazis and criminals are interchangeable.

Princess Lavinia and Lulu Bell offer an interesting contrast of the old world and the new. Princess Lavinia is a Russian aristocrat in exile, driven out of her world by the Russian Revolution in 1917. Lulu Bell offers a perspective on the possibilities of the new world toward which the whole plane is headed. As an actress, Lulu represents the new aristocracy, those people who attain wealth and privilege by virtue of their celebrity rather than by their inherited title or successful business achievements. Lulu is notable to the other passengers, among other things, for the fact that she looks to be about forty years old in person but nineteen years old on screen. The contrast between the old world that cannot maintain its order and the new world that invests so heavily in building fictional orders suggests the ambiguity about the choices the passengers are making.

Plot Development

The novel opens on the day World War II was declared, placing the action in an important historical context. The first chapter sets the story in motion by introducing the plane itself and a shadowy figure, Tom

Luther, who the reader understands is engaged in a plot against someone who is to take the flight. Tom's mission is the force that drives the plot. Its resolution pulls together all the smaller intrigues of the other passengers.

The first stage in the action unfolds with a phone call to Eddie Deakin, the flight engineer, ordering him to force the plane down into an emergency landing just before arriving in New York and threatening to rape and kill his wife, whom the unidentified caller has kidnapped. Eddie's effort to manipulate the plane's flight pattern adds suspense because an error on his part could mean the plane's destruction and his wife's death.

The Oxenford family is in flight from England because of the unpopular pro-Nazi politics of Lord Oxenford. Also fleeing England is a jewel thief, Harry Marks, whose attraction to Margaret Oxenford and to her mother's jewels pulls him into the family dynamics. Diana Lovesey, an unhappy wife, is fleeing from Mervyn, her boring husband, to a new life in America with her lover, Mark Alder. Nancy Lenehan, an American businesswoman, is racing back to America to save her share of the family business. Her chance meeting with Mervyn Lovesey as they both race to catch the plane leads to a romantic relationship.

The action of *Night over Water* is divided into six parts, each of which contains five chapters (except Part 6, which has four). Each part is equivalent to one stage of the journey. The novel's main plot device, the threat to Eddie Deakin, is set in motion early but leaves unclear the specific target of the kidnap attempt. Because Tom Luther is American, like the voices Eddie hears on the phone, Eddie concludes that the thugs are after the gangster Frankie Giordino, who is being escorted back to the States by an FBI agent. That remains the premise for the rest of the book until the true target of the kidnappers is revealed at the end. The lengthy series of steps that Eddie must perform in order to pull off his task keeps the reader engaged in the action, especially since each step involves risk of discovery for Eddie and risk to all the passengers if his calculations are even the slightest bit off.

The phone call to Eddie makes him a spy on his own plane. Like a spy he must operate without detection in a hostile area. His actions create tension because the reader knows that his wife's life is on the line. Tom, who is in fact the spy on board, comes under no suspicion and is in no danger of being exposed. The other interloper on the plane is Harry Marks, who snoops around the overhead luggage compartments in the hopes of finding Lady Oxenford's jewels.

The kidnapping of the person Tom wants is the overarching structuring agent in the novel, but it is not the major action. That is devoted to the series of romantic subplots and the attempt at independence by Margaret Oxenford and Harry Marks.

Thematic Issues

Night over Water has two major themes: the need to recognize the danger of the totalitarian threat to democracy and the unjust treatment of women by men and by World War II-era society. The book assumes that the reader accepts totalitarianism and sexism as dangerous and evil. It suggests, however, that people who have not actively addressed these evils may contribute to their continuation.

Many characters show a lack of understanding of the threat of Nazism. Margaret Oxenford represents the best example of what a lack of knowledge can do. Her sentiments are deeply and thoroughly liberal, but her lack of education prevents her from understanding the monstrous positions her father takes. As she gains knowledge, she is able to reject his politics and his opinions on race and class. Similarly, Harry Marks ignores political events by myopically focusing on his greed. In fact, had he decided to keep out of sight in order to secure the jewels, the thugs might have won after all. Lady Oxenford's passive acceptance of all that happens within elite circles suggests a blindness to real evil and immediate danger. Mark Alder's isolationism suggests the myopia of people who see only their short-range goals. His willingness to tolerate Nazis as long as they do not attack something close to him is undercut when the thugs decide to take Diana with them as a sexual trophy. Baron Gabon argues that tolerance in a complex world means more than just accepting other people. It means taking active measures to promote tolerance. Margaret's rejection of her father's use of "civilized" challenges the reader to make a commitment to tolerance and decency. The failure of aristocrats as world leaders and the unacceptableness of the alternatives offered by ideologues suggest that ordinary citizens must rise to the occasion and seize the reins of leadership in a world where institutions are changing and traditional allegiances are being questioned.

Harry Marks's facility with accents and his success at intermingling with aristocratic groups illustrates the threat of Nazis and gangsters to aristocratic privilege. If the aristocrats themselves cannot identify a pretender in their own midst, then, the novel suggests, they have lost their claims on privilege. Like George Bernard Shaw's *Pygmalion*, the novel presents a person who can pass for an aristocrat by imitating the accent and dress. Although Harry has some tight moments in fooling Lady Oxenford about the details of American aristocrats, he manages to learn the lessons of class well enough to turn class prejudice to his own ends and against the aristocrats themselves.

The other major theme is the injustices facing women at that time. The inadequacy of Margaret's education and her lack of sophistication show how little women count even in the most elite circles. Margaret regrets that her mother is so passive and wishes that they could come to some agreement not to let men treat them as decorations. Mervyn Lovesey treats his wife's requests for respect and consideration as the requests of a child. He pays so little attention to Diana that he is oblivious to her summer-long affair and might have missed her departure on the plane had she not left a note. He deprecates her voice and needs and expects her to show the passivity and docility exhibited by Lady Oxenford. Nancy Lenehan runs into sexist assumptions in her business dealings even though she has a long and successful business record. She has to demand respect and recognition from Mervyn. In the course of the novel, Margaret, Diana, and Nancy find ways to assert themselves. In the end each finds both a satisfying relationship with a man and personal independence. Diana makes a choice to pursue her own happiness without regard to what Mervyn or others expect her to do. Nancy finds a way to stay in business and move to England with Mervyn. And Margaret is at the controls of the launch as she and Harry head toward the Canadian border and a new life together.

Literary Devices

Like other Follett novels, *Night over Water* uses similes to advantage. The plane taking off is compared to a racehorse jumping a fence (176), and the plane landing is compared to a Mallard duck (7). Carl Hartmann appears to Margaret as being as thin as death (143). Follett also uses allusion clearly. In the opening chapter Tom Luther hums some bars of Beethoven's *Emperor* concerto and thinks about how it seems to be sufficiently warlike for him. The reader is not likely to think much of this detail at the time because there is no reason to expect that Luther is anything other than an American interested in the plane. But the end of the novel reveals this detail as an allusion to Luther's German allegiance.

Another allusion in that same chapter does in fact alert the reader to

Luther's German allegiance, but it is clear only to readers of *Eye of the Needle*. In that novel the spy who causes all the trouble is named Henry Faber. Faber is the person who tells Luther that the man he wants will be on the plane. Since the action of *Eye of the Needle* begins in 1940, it is likely that Faber might have been available for such an assignment in September 1939. The allusion is a stretch for all except Follett fans. Follett has included such details from his other novels in other books, but none so central to the action.

The most extensively developed literary device in the novel is the connection, in Harry Marks' mind, between jewelry and sexual activity. The first reference is actually an ironic juxtaposition; the reader knows that Harry has been thinking about stealing jewels when Margaret tells him that he looks as if he is thinking about someone he loves:

> Harry knew he would never again be this close to such a masterpiece. Never. He had to steal it. The risks were appalling—but then, he had always been lucky. "I don't believe you're listening to me," Margaret said. Harry realized he had not been paying attention. He grinned and said: "I'm sorry. Something you said sent me into a daydream." "I know," she said. "From the look on your face, you were dreaming about someone you love." (173)

The contrast between the criminal act he was actually thinking about and the delicate sentiment that Margaret attributes to him is humorous and it introduces the connection Harry frequently makes between jewelry and passion. Later in the novel, immediately after he has spent the night with Margaret, Harry's thoughts connect their night together to her mother's jewels: "He longed to hold that necklace in his hands, feast his eyes on the fathomless red of the Burmese rubies, and run his fingertips over the faceted diamonds" (386). The tactile pleasure of jewels takes on a sexual connotation. Weighing the decision to steal the jewels and lose Margaret or give up the jewels in the hope of winning her, he makes the connection explicit: "But he was wondering whether Margaret's breasts were not the most precious jewels he would ever hold" (387). Later in the novel he imagines Margaret with nothing on except the jewels and the thought stimulates him. The equation of jewelry and sexual passion highlights the conflict he faces between greed and love. Because Harry is a jewel thief, giving up this life will be a great sacrifice. Although the reader can easily see that giving up the jewels for Margaret is the right choice, Harry's background and personality make such a choice very difficult for him. This defining moment in Harry's life is dramatized beautifully by Follett's use of language to equate jewelry and sexual passion.

A PLACE CALLED FREEDOM

A Place Called Freedom is a historical romance, but it also draws on elements of the family saga and the thriller that have been the hallmarks of Ken Follett's fiction. Geographically, the story ranges across Great Britain and then across the Atlantic to colonial Virginia, although, unlike Follett's sagas, it takes place within a single year, 1767. Like the Pilasters in *A Dangerous Fortune*, the Jamissons are a wealthy merchant family, although they have already acquired the title and ancestral lands to which Augusta Pilaster aspired. Unlike the Pilasters, and more like the Hamleighs of *The Pillars of the Earth*, the Jamissons are a thoroughly bad lot. They symbolize the worst excesses of power, wealth, and aristocratic privilege.

The political and economic upheavals of the late eighteenth century, including the American and French revolutions, undercut the aristocratic privilege the Jamissons have sought so eagerly and replaced it with capitalism and a government and a society based on individual rights. Follett's novel defines those ideas of freedom, liberty, and the pursuit of happiness and develops a story that sketches out how these principles operate and win in eighteenth-century America and in the modern world.

The story of *A Place Called Freedom* begins with an independent-minded coal miner's protest against the virtual slavery imposed on miners in Scotland. For his protest Malachi ("Mack") McAsh is brutally punished and then allowed to escape to prevent him from stirring up further trouble in the mining village. Mack's protest catches the attention of Lizzie Hallim, a beautiful and spirited aristocrat who lives on an estate adjoining the Jamisson lands, where the mines are located. Because Lizzie's family has lost its wealth, she agrees to marry Jay Jamisson, the younger son. Jay's mother convinces her husband to give Jay and Lizzie a plantation in Virginia as a wedding present.

Having fled to London, Mack struggles to earn a living and finds regular work loading coal on to ships. Rebelling against the unjust working conditions, he organizes a strike against the shipowners and their agents.

The Jamissons, who own some of these ships, conspire with the government to break the strike by provoking a riot and attacking the striking workers. Jay Jamisson, a captain in the Horse Guard, leads the troops against the strikers and arrests many, including Mack. Lizzie, who has been living in London in preparation for the move to Virginia, influences her husband to reduce his charges against Mack. Mack is sentenced to transportation to America and is herded on to a ship headed for Virginia, the same ship, it turns out, that Lizzie and Jay will take.

In Virginia Mack is indentured to Jay's plantation. The ordinary life on the plantation increases Mack's connections with Lizzie. As Jay's dissipation in his new setting alienates Lizzie, she grows closer to Mack. The couple finally runs away from Jay and his henchmen and make a break for the wilderness west of Virginia. Jay chases them and the confrontation between Jay and Lizzie is the climax of the novel. Mack and Lizzie establish a new life in the new and open society of the new world.

Point of View

A Place Called Freedom begins with a common narrative strategy, although Ken Follett has not used it previously. The novel opens with the short account of a twentieth-century narrator about finding an iron collar. The narrator's informal, matter-of-fact tone creates a sense of authenticity and honesty and ends with the disingenuous "If the iron collar could talk, I think to myself, what kind of story would it tell?" (iii). As it happens, the next pages announce a long story that begins in Scotland in 1767 and ends less than a year later in America. The twentieth-century account operates primarily as a jumping off point for the story. Follett could have started his story in any number of equally artificial ways, but this device ultimately contributes to the thematic and ideological concerns of the novel. Anticipating the question of why someone would buy a dilapidated house far out in the country, the narrator of this opening section offers only a vague, "I just love this valley" (i), but the terms he then uses to specify what he loves about it echo (in retrospect, of course) what Malachi McAsh, the main hero of the novel, says he loves about his homeland and what he looks for in the new land he finally reaches. Their similar attraction to the land suggests a continuity in human values over time that often appears in Follett's novels.

The narrator's eagerness to work on his land and its buildings himself offers another perspective on the thematic and structural aspects of the novel. For him, work is healthy and rewarding, a voluntary act that is almost a hobby. This attitude introduces the subject of work and its rewards, which becomes a major theme in the novel.

As in other Follett novels, the narrator is omniscient, but the perspective is limited to one character at a time. The point of view shifts among the three main characters, Mack McAsh, Lizzie Hallim (later Jamisson), and Jay Jamisson. Most of the chapters are seen through the perspective of one of these three characters. For a few chapters the point of view shifts within the chapter. The issues and values of the novel are defined and articulated in the thoughts and opinions of these three characters.

Character Development

Mack McAsh stands out as the most dominant character in the novel. Mack is introduced as an independent thinker who is fiercely protective of his freedom. The first chapter focuses on his ability to read and write, which was unusual for that time, and the tradition of challenge and argumentation fostered by his family. These traits reflect Enlightenment ideas about individual rights and democratic participation in social and political structures. During the novel Mack twice attributes his interest and skill in arguing to his experiences in the make-shift tavern established in Mrs. Whiegel's parlor. This tavern is a working-class version of the coffee houses and clubs where Enlightenment ideas of freedom and individual rights germinated. Speaking out in public comes naturally and by habit to Mack. Standing up to aristocratic privilege, he becomes the clear hero in the novel.

He also becomes a hero to those around him. In Scotland the miners have trusted him with the important task of taking care of them and the mine when a dangerous level of gas accumulates in it. When he stands up to the lord of the manor and is punished for it, the people rally around him and recognize his leadership and his sacrifice even though there is little they can do to help him. Even the lord recognizes his power—he allows Mack to run away to be rid of him so that he will no longer create resistance and, in the lord's eyes, trouble. Mack rises to the same kind of leadership position in London by leading the exploited coal haulers in rebellion against the bosses who keep them in the same kind of poverty and dependence Mack had left in Scotland. He assumes leadership of a movement that addresses the injustices of capitalism and of the political system, and his personal integrity becomes identifiable with the beginnings of liberal democratic systems in Europe and America. Mack's identification with the stories and myths of the founding fathers contributes to his standing as a hero. But he is not just the embodiment of democratic ideals; he is also a reflective and considerate human being. He changes in small ways and grows more tolerant and considerate as the novel progresses, but his character remains essentially stable throughout the novel.

Lizzie Hallim, the second important character in the novel, is characterized by her curiosity, her passionate insistence on being treated as an intelligent equal, and her integrity in dealing with people. She is an aristocrat, but her family's estate has fallen on hard times and she is forced to consider marriage to shore up her family's fortunes and ensure that her mother will be able to keep High Glen, the estate she has known since childhood. She dutifully agrees to marry Robert Jamisson for his family's money, although she clearly reflects on the plusses and minuses of the alliance. Her mother worries about Lizzie's impulsiveness, and her strong and aggressive behavior continually evokes surprise and the suggestion that she is not "ladylike." The reader comes to recognize this unconventional behavior as a mark of Lizzie's best qualities, her version of Mack's stubborn and insistent integrity. Lizzie's willingness to reach beyond expected or conventional behavior is emphasized by the repeated incidents in which she dresses as a man. In response to Mack's challenge about knowledge of the mine, she dons male attire and goes down to the mine with Jay Jamisson. She does the same when she wants to see Mack's boxing match and later his trial in London. Each of Lizzie's disguises raises issues about gender roles in eighteenth-century society. After the mine adventure, Lizzie's mother warns her that such behavior diminishes her chances for finding a husband. The episode at the boxing match explicitly addresses the anomalies in access to power between the sexes: "She went into the tavern, banged on the counter with a fist, and said to the barman: 'A pint of strong ale, Jack.' It was wonderful to address the world in such arrogant tones. If she did the same in women's clothing, every man she spoke to would feel entitled to reprove her, even tavern keepers and sedan-chairmen. But a pair of breeches was a licence to command" (122). From the novel's beginning she resists the pressure to ride sidesaddle and otherwise conform to the secondary status of well-bred ladies. Her interest in changing dress becomes an emblem of her resistance toward societal restrictions.

Lizzie is also generous and faithful. She pays special attention to Mack in the beginning because she remembers him and his twin sister, Esther, from their childhood days. Her reactions to the suffering of the poor puts her at odds with her fellow aristocrats, and her attachment to the beauty and integrity of the land, which causes her to oppose mining, leads to her first conflict with her husband. Lizzie's path constantly crosses Mack's in a series of coincidental meetings, which lead to her increasing interest in him.

Lizzie's husband, Jay Jamisson, the third major character, provides the other point of view of the action. Early on, the reader, after identifying with Lizzie and Mack, learns to despise and then fear Jay's cruel and narrow pursuit of pleasure and his own interests. As the novel proceeds, Jay's character develops into a stereotype of a decadent aristocrat. The irony implicit in this stereotype is that Jay and his family are brand new aristocrats, without a family history of aristocratic decadence, his father having married into the title and the lands. Although Jay has grown up with money, his own vicious tastes seem to be the source of his collection of aristocratic vices. His father and his older brother are defined very much by their mercantile interests and abilities; Jay stands out as the aristocrat in bearing and interests, although he lacks an understanding of the responsibilities traditionally associated with aristocratic privilege.

The opening of the novel presents Jay in his best light, perhaps so that the reader can believe that Lizzie might have some reason for being interested in him. The occasion for the family's return to their estate in Scotland is to orchestrate the engagement of Jay's older brother to Lizzie and to celebrate Jay's twenty-first birthday. On that occasion Jay is charming enough to interest Lizzie. The subsequent events in the opening section show him to be vicious enough to want to kill his brother in order to replace him as heir to the estate and weak enough to follow the direction of his mother in developing a scheme to get some kind of settlement from his father. In order to avoid the discomfort of his father's anger over his taking Lizzie down into the mine, he betrays Mack's intention to leave his servitude and so is responsible for the severe punishment that Mack endures at the hands of Sir George Jamisson. Jay is responsible for Mack's entrapment in London as well and his motives again reveal him as weak and self-indulgent.

His character stops short of total villainy only because he is too weak and contemptible to be completely wicked. His impulses are focused entirely on dissipation and vanity. After he moves to America with Lizzie, he tells her that he has no intention of becoming a farmer and enters immediately on a plan to become a leading citizen in the colonial government, an ambition the reader knows is foolish because he has already shown himself to be ignorant of local conditions and insensitive to the interests of his fellow colonialists. The reader has no misgivings about Lizzie's increasing dislike of him and her decision to leave him and follow Mack. By the end of the novel, Jay is chasing his wife, who has run off with Mack, but his motive is not jealousy or rage. After his father's death, his mother came to America and brought him word that in order to receive a portion of his father's inheritance he must either force Lizzie to have a child by him very soon or arrange for her death so that he can marry someone else who will produce a grandchild. Jay is willing to see Lizzie dead but squeamish about killing her himself, just as earlier in the novel he is full of bravado about marching on a mob to maintain order but fearful about getting into the actual fight. In the end the reader is glad to see him get his just deserts.

Jay's father and his brother, Robert, are equally unlikable characters, although as villains both are less complex and less interesting than Jay. Neither has Jay's charm and interest in traditional aristocratic vices. Both are driven by mercantile interests and see the world almost entirely in terms of money and power. Although Sir George has a title, he never strays very far from being a ruthless, narrow-minded businessman. He clearly adopts aristocratic values in exercising authority and suppressing new ideas on liberty and democratic participation in government, but he never loses sight of his business interests. Robert is, if anything, a more intense version of his father's driving greed and business ruthlessness and seems to differ only in that he lacks his father's sentimental fondness for his wives. Like many eighteenth-century landed gentry, Robert regards marriage as an occasion for building family fortunes. His anger on learning that Lizzie has chosen Jay instead of him seems to arise more from a wounded sense of pride and regret at having lost access to Lizzie's lands than from a sense of loss of someone he loved. Sir George, Robert, and the rest of the Jamisson family become even more distasteful when they fall to arguing among themselves. The family squabbles show a group of completely unlikable people who differ only in the manner and quality of their vile traits.

Jay's mother, Alicia, stands out from the rest because she is devious and clever. Like the biblical Rebecca, Isaac's wife, who advises her son Jacob on how to cheat his brother Esau out of his patrimony, Alicia constructs the plans that enable Jay to surmount his own weaknesses. Jay does not win the patrimony, but he does take his brother's intended bride and some of his father's wealth. Alicia seems faithful only to Jay and is uninterested in his wife except as Lizzie is able to advance Jay's fortune. She bears some resemblance to the clever and ambitious matrons Lady Hamleigh in *Pillars of the Earth* and Augusta Pilaster in A *Dangerous Fortune*. Alicia is a formidable villain and one of Follett's strong female characters because of her cleverness and her fierce determination.

Plot Development

A Place Called Freedom begins in Virginia in the 1990s and then steps back in time to the mining village of Heugh, Scotland, in the 1760s. The main events of the novel—a challenge to arbitrary authority, punishment, and flight—repeat themselves, forming an episodic structure. In the last chapter of the novel, Mack dreams about the wilderness west of Virginia toward which he is heading as "a place called freedom," and so the title of the novel is realized at the very end. His commitment to freedom and the principles of individual rights and democratic systems is present from the opening chapter and drives the action of the novel.

The episodes that make up the bulk of the novel involve Mack's attempt to defend his intrinsic worth and the repeated denial of that worth by the ruling aristocrats. Each time he asserts himself he is punished far beyond any reasonable degree or ordinary interpretation of the law by members of the Jamisson family. The novel makes clear, however, that other aristocrats might have done the same thing and that it is coincidence and local circumstance that make the Jamissons the constant threat. As the agents of retribution, the Jamissons pursue Mack as he seeks to escape oppression. Capitalists and irresponsible aristocrats, the Jamissons represent what is wrong with eighteenth-century political and social systems.

Each of the three sections of the book opens with Mack in servitude of some kind but ready to assert his independence whenever circumstances tread on his sense of justice or threaten his friends or family. In Scotland, his challenge to Sir George Jamisson's right to enslave miners creates the confrontation for which Mack is severely punished and then allowed to run away. In London, his challenge to Sidney Lennox, a coal boss, leads him to organize the coal haulers, threaten the flow of coal to London, and earn the wrath of the ruling class. He is entrapped and punished again, this time by being sent to America in bondage. In Virginia, the twin evils of a system that leaves a young girl at the mercy of her purchaser and enables a husband like Jay to treat his horses better than his wife combine to push Mack into defying his servitude and taking flight once again. In this third flight his decision is shared by Lizzie, who has helped him in his first flight and provided him with support during his second flight. The location changes, but the conflicts are essentially the same. The attacks on Mack become more personal and more vicious as the novel proceeds, and his responses become more seasoned and sophisticated. Confinement marks each location: the small village where Mack spends most of his time in the mine; the tumult of bustling London where he works in the holds of coal ships, lives with a friend in an overcrowded apartment, and spends his life in crowded taverns or mob-filled streets; and the voyage to America in a ship's hold, where he cannot sit up straight, and is allowed to walk around for only a short time once a day. After all that confinement, Mack finds America a place of openness, a change that is immediately perceptible and welcome. He finds out, however, that bondage is still intolerable even when the physical surroundings do not keep him penned in and that the system established by the slaveholders keeps slaves confined without any physical fence or cell. At the end, as Mack and Lizzie run from Jay, they are running to reach both a real and symbolic open place beyond the mountains, and that final race releases them from the confinement that has shaped so much of the action of the novel.

Thematic Issues

Other Follett novels encourage readers to think about values and concerns of importance to them individually. But *A Place Called Freedom* directs readers to think about values and assumptions of Western democratic institutions. Here Follett posits individual rights against capitalistic imperatives. Mack represents and often articulates the democratic tenet that all people are created equal and should have the opportunity to live in freedom and dignity. The exchanges among the aristocrats, which suggest that miners do not feel pain in the same way that aristocrats do or that members of an urban mob are best regarded as nuisances to be dispatched with less regard than if they were animals, reflect the dominant attitudes at the time, which denied freedom and dignity to certain classes. Although she has been raised as an aristocrat, Lizzie Hallim espouses democratic values too. She has escaped the insensitivity of her class because she has had contact with the people whom she is asked to dismiss. This experience fosters her independence, which leads to her declaration of love for Mack and her belief in the

value of people, not privilege. Lizzie merits the reader's approval because she is able to reject aristocratic privilege in favor of democratic
values.

Follett uses the Jamisson family to castigate both the institution of
aristocratic privilege and the primacy of wealth that often supplants aristocracy as the source of power in the Western world. Having gained
entry to society through mercantile success and fortune, members of the
family emulate the actions and attitudes of the landed aristocracy. That
the transfer of power from the aristocracy to the capitalists was so easy
reveals the hypocrisy of the social structure. The novel takes a skeptical
view of the pretensions of successful capitalists to the blessings of power
and privilege that accompanied the titles that they bought with their
newly acquired fortunes. So the novel condemns these sources of power
and suggests that the forces of democracy that finally prevailed in the
late eighteenth, nineteenth, and twentieth centuries did so by overcoming strong and well-endowed resistance from aristocratic and capitalistic traditions.

This version of how democracy works ignores the degree to which
democracy owes its inception to mercantile interests and the tenets of
capitalism. Twentieth-century views of the origins of democracy may
identify more with grassroots movements than with the celebration of
individualism that spawned both capitalism and democracy, but the emphasis in *A Place Called Freedom* is clearly on the abuses perpetrated by
both the aristocracy and the mercantile class who have dominated European and American society since the Enlightenment.

Like many other Follett novels, *Place* asks that readers think about the
roles of women. In eighteenth-century English society Lizzie Hallim is
not taken seriously because as a woman she is expected to abide by rules
that restrict her behavior. She certainly shows how much effort it takes
for a woman to follow her own instincts and her own ideas of right and
wrong. The novel focuses on gender roles by repeatedly putting Lizzie
into situations where she has to dress as a man in order to follow her
heart or her conscience. She enjoys the challenge of wearing men's
clothes and temporarily exercising male power and prerogative, but the
ambiguity created by her disguises emphasizes the extent of the duality
in standards for men and for women of that day.

Literary Devices

A Place Called Freedom is one of Follett's most self-consciously crafted novels. The voice from the present that triggers a story from the past is an artificial device that ties the action of the novel to modern life. The artifacts found on the property in America are left unidentified and become recognizable as Mack's history unfolds. The collar symbolizes the shackles that Mack fought so hard to unlock. The revelation that the book found in the box at the New World site of High Glen was Daniel Defoe's *Robinson Crusoe* resists easy application to the situation depicted in the novel. Crusoe is certainly a model of self-reliance and independence, but Defoe repeatedly attributes Crusoe's success to God's providence, while Follett's novel never seems to nod at providential intervention.

A Place Called Freedom frequently alludes to other novels. It comments amusedly on the genre in noting that Lizzie has a novel in her lap that cannot keep her attention. The narrator mentions that Lizzie likes adventure novels and cites three noted eighteenth-century examples. (It is interesting to note that Follett feels compelled to describe the three as "all stories of adventure" because he cannot depend upon his reader's recognition of the works.) The novel's emphasis on reading and participating in public discussion about important political and cultural issues begins in the first chapter and returns at regular intervals. The Jamissons do not read, either for business or for pleasure, but other minor characters see reading and writing as a key to liberation and greater access to the Enlightenment's promises of life, liberty, and the pursuit of happiness.

Lord Archer's Coffeehouse, a central location in the London section of the novel and the name of an actual eighteenth-century London coffeehouse, is a tongue-in-cheek reference to a twentieth-century fellow English novelist, Jeffrey Archer, who has recently been knighted and so is now Lord Archer. In a novel that features a bitter rivalry between two brothers, Follett's glance at Jeffrey Archer also encourages the reader to remember that one of Archer's most successful novels is *Cain and Abel*.

Jay Jamisson's sure observation that the colonists cannot succeed in their plans to separate from England amounts to dramatic irony, since the reader shares with the author the knowledge that the colonists will indeed be successful and that young royalists like Jay suffered extensively in the war's aftermath. Other occasions also reveal the hollowness of Jay's thinking, especially about Lizzie. His concern about his horse on the sea journey is juxtaposed with the absence of his concern about Lizzie's comfort and well-being, and he thinks about his victory in getting Lizzie to agree to something as a winning hand in a card game.

A READER-RESPONSE APPROACH TO *NIGHT OVER WATER* AND *A PLACE CALLED FREEDOM*

Reader-response criticism begins from the assumption that the meaning of a literary work is created by the interaction of the reader and the text. It posits that literary experience begins in the reader's subjective interpretation of the text based on the experiences and perceptions he or she brings to it. In other words, the reader fills in the gaps in the text and this active participation is a crucial part of the literary experience. Reader-response critics balance the specific dynamics of a reader's active appropriation of a text with recognizable structures in the text and define meaning as the product of this interaction. The reader is thus a partner with the writer in creating the meaning of the work. Drawing on psychoanalytical theory, some reader-response critics see the reader as imposing meaning on the words, meaning that is shaped as much by the reader's psychological needs and desires as by the rhetorical strategies of the writer. Reader-response criticism has also been defined in terms of the social and cultural conventions that readers as a group bring to a text based on a community of broad or local values. Texts can also be understood in terms of reader responses in different eras.

Both *Night over Water* and *A Place Called Freedom* are accessible through reader-response techniques. Occurring in a closed space, the events of *Night over Water* might seem to leave little to the reader's imagination. But the novel relies on the reader's responses to connect the action in the plane with the events in England, Europe, and America. The novel leaves implicit, rather than explicit, references to the rising tide of Nazism and the tensions over the response to it on both sides of the Atlantic because the reader has a general knowledge of the events surrounding World War II as well as shared values about the meaning of those events. Some readers also have knowledge of specific events that enhances the reading of the text, and they attribute values to the concerns at stake in the novel. The author can depend upon readers to bring these attitudes and knowledge of events to the reading because the author, the reader, and many of the characters in the novel belong to a community that shares many values and assumptions about life as well as interest in novels and an understanding of the English language. Reader-response approaches to texts examine the shared assumptions between reader and writer in creating the meaning of the text.

A Place Called Freedom illustrates how the formal elements of the text anticipate and build upon reader responses. The opening section presents a voice of a recognizable, twentieth-century American who represents the American reading public—at least of Follett's novels. The reader identifies with the upwardly mobile, apparently financially successful and socially respectable narrator and adopts the narrator's perspective on the events that follow. The reader can easily accept this role because it is familiar. The specific construction of meaning a reader develops may begin from this common recognition, but it is more likely that this recognition will offer insight into the experience of reading this text as the reader fills in the connections with personal perspectives. For instance, the discovery of a slave's collar presents an easily recognizable symbol to most readers and points to issues of personal liberty and human dignity that will dominate the novel. From the beginning the reader is positioned to separate characters and events into acceptable or offensive according to the terms introduced very early. But individual readers will concretize this symbol based on their personal experiences and background. Each reader's experiences enriches the range and meaning of the text.

Although each reader imposes his or her own meaning on the text, American readers bring shared assumptions to this creation of meaning. The political and social developments of the late eighteenth century—especially the American and French revolutions, the new interest in turning America into its own nation, and the Industrial Revolution—provide the foundations for the American reader's shared political and social values and traditions. America's continuing commitment to open democratic processes and to pursuit of an egalitarian society assumes that readers will identify with the overthrow of political, social, and economic hierarchies depicted in the novel. Although readers of *A Place Called Freedom* will differ widely in their specific political, social, and economic loyalties and experiences, they see themselves as still engaged in the democratic process. Present-day opponents of democracy may appear different from the aristocrats and swindlers portrayed in the novel, but they still represent a challenge to the principle that requires individuals to rise to the challenge of opposition. Late twentieth-century readers may not face the cruel physical punishments Mack endures, but they also risk loss of property and personal liberty if they do not challenge the special ideological or business interests ready to subvert democratic processes. The reader's response to *A Place Called Freedom* is likely to be enriched by the democratic heritage that reinforces the values that operate in the novel.

Bibliography

Note: Page numbers referred to in the text are to the paperback editions of Ken Follett's works.

WORKS BY KEN FOLLETT

The Bear Raid. London: Harwood-Smart, 1976.
"Capitalism, Socialism, and Radio WAWA." *Bookseller*, 18 September 1992: 826.
A Dangerous Fortune. New York: Delacorte Press, 1993.
Eye of the Needle. Macdonald and Jane's, 1978. New York: Arbor House, 1978. Published in England as *Storm Island*.
"Fall from Grace." *New York Times Book Review*, 16 June 1985: 14.
The Heist of the Century, with "Rene Louis Maurice." London: Fontana, 1978. Published in the United States as *The Gentlemen of 16 July*. New York: Arbor House, 1980. Revised edition published as *Under the Streets of Nice: The Bank Heist of the Century*. New York: National Press, 1986.
"Keeping the Plot Turning." *Bookseller* 8 September 1995: 68–69.
The Key to Rebecca. New York: William Morrow, 1980.
Lie Down with Lions. New York: William Morrow, 1986.
The Man from St. Petersburg. New York: William Morrow, 1982.
Night over Water. New York: William Morrow, 1991.
On Wings of Eagles. New York: William Morrow, 1983 (nonfiction).
The Pillars of the Earth. New York: William Morrow, 1989.

A Place Called Freedom. New York: Crown Publishers, 1995.

The Secret of Kellerman's Studio. London: Abelard-Schuman, 1976. Published in the United States as *The Mystery Hideout.* New York: William Morrow, 1990.

"The Spy as Hero and Villain." In *The Murder Mystique: Crime Writers on Their Work.* Ed. Lucy Freeman. New York: Ungar, 1980.

Triple. London: Macdonald, 1979.

The Shakeout. London: Harwood-Smart, 1975.

Writing as "Martin Martinsen"

The Power Twins and the Worm Puzzle. London: Abelard-Schuman, 1976.

Writing as "Symon Myles"

The Big Black. London: Everest Books, 1974.

The Big Hit. London: Everest Books, 1975.

The Big Needle. London: Everest Books, 1974. Published in the United States as *The Big Apple.* New York: Kensington, 1975, and later reissued under its original title under Ken Follett's name.

Writing as "Bernard L. Ross"

Amok: King of Legend. London: Futura, 1976.

Capricorn One. Based on the screenplay by Peter Hyams. London: Futura, 1978.

Writing as "Zachary Stone"

The Modigliani Scandal. London: Collins, 1976. Published in the United States under Ken Follett's name by Penguin Books in 1985.

Paper Money. London: Collins, 1977. Published in the United States under Ken Follett's name by Penguin Books in 1987.

WORKS ABOUT KEN FOLLETT

Dictionary of Literary Biography. Vol. 87, *British Mystery and Thriller Writers Since 1940,* 1st Series. New York: Gale, 1989.

Dictionary of Literary Biography Yearbook: 1981. New York: Gale, 1982.
Magill, Frank N., ed. *Critical Survey of Mystery and Detective Fiction.* Englewood
    Cliffs, N.J.: Salem Press, 1988.
Moritz, Charles, ed. *Current Biography Yearbook 1990.* New York: H. W. Wilson
    Company, 1990.
Ramet, Carlos. "Ken Follett from Start to Finish: The Transformation of a Writer."
    Studies in Popular Culture 15, 2 (1993): 79-86.
Reilly, John M., ed. *Twentieth-Century Crime and Mystery Writers*, 2nd ed. New
    York: St. Martin's Press, 1985.

INTERVIEWS WITH KEN FOLLETT

Ken Follett, interviewed by the author by phone, 22 May 1995, Indianapolis, IN.
Ken Follett, interviewed by Jean W. Ross. "CA Interview." In *Contemporary Au-
    thors*, New Revision Series, Vol. 33. Ed. James G. Lesniak. New York: Gale,
    1991.
Ken Follett, interviewed by John R. Baker. "PW Interviews Ken Follett." *Publish-
    er's Weekly*, 17 January 1986: 54-55.
Ken Follett, "Feedback." *Bon Appetit*, 1 February 1995: 134.

REVIEWS AND CRITICISM

Eye of the Needle

Book World-The Washington Post, 2 July 1978: F1, F4.
Saturday Review, August 1978: 51.

Triple

Nation, 26 April 1980: 504-6.
New York Times Book Review, 21 September 1980: 9

The Key to Rebecca

Nation, 20 December 1980: 677.
New York, 12 January 1981: 52.
Newsweek, 29 September 1980: 83.

People Weekly, 13 October 1980: 18.
Time, 29 September 1980: 88.

The Man from St. Petersburg

Library Bulletin, September 1982: 63.
Maclean's, 14 June 1982: 55.
New Yorker, 16 August 1982: 93.
People Weekly, 7 June 1982: 14.
Time, 3 May 1982: 76.
Ramet, Carlos. "Unification and Evaporation in *The Man from St. Petersburg*." *Clues: A Journal of Detection* 9, 2 (fall-winter 1988): 63-73.
Newsweek, 2 October 1983: 80.
New Republic, 13 July 1992: 12.

The Modigliani Scandal

New York Times Book Review, 30 June 1985: 16.
Art in America, July 1986: 15.
The New Yorker, 8 July 1985: 75.

Lie Down with Lions

Library Journal, 1 February 1986: 92.
New York Times Book Review, 26 January 1986: 9.
People Weekly, 17 February 1986: 23.
Publisher's Weekly, 13 December 1985: 44.
Time, 24 February 1986: 76.

Paper Money

Publisher's Weekly, 21 August 1987: 55.

The Pillars of the Earth

Library Journal, 15 April 1989: 60.
Library Journal, July 1989: 108.
New York Times Book Review, 16 June 1989: 14.
New York Times Book Review, 10 September 1989: 41.
Publisher's Weekly, 30 June 1989: 86.

Night over Water

New York Times Book Review, 29 September 1991: 22.

A Dangerous Fortune

New York Times Book Review, 9 January 1994: 19.
Publisher's Weekly, 23 August 1993: 57.

A Place Called Freedom

Library Journal, August 1995: 115.
New York Times Book Review, 14 January 1996: 19.
Publisher's Weekly, 5 June 1995: 48.

OTHER SECONDARY SOURCES

Andersson, Theodore M. "The Icelandic Sagas." In *Heroic Epic and Saga*. Ed. Felix J. Oinas. Bloomington: Indiana University Press, 1978.

Bargainer, Earl, ed. *Twelve Englishmen of Mystery*. Bowling Green, Ohio: Bowling Green University Press, 1984.

Cawelti, John G., and Bruce A. Rosenberg. *The Spy Story*. Chicago: University of Chicago Press, 1987.

Cassiday, Bruce, ed. *Modern Mystery, Fantasy, and Science Fiction Writers*. New York: Continuum, 1993.

Contemporary Authors, New Revision Series, Vol. 33. Ed. James G. Lesniak. New York: Gale, 1991.

Contemporary Literary Criticism, Vol. 18. Ed. Sharon Ganton. New York: Gale, 1981.

Dove, George N. *Suspense in the Formula Story*. Bowling Green, Ohio: Bowling Green University Press, 1989.

Grossvogel, David I. *Mystery and Its Fictions: From Oedipus to Agatha Christie*. Baltimore: Johns Hopkins University Press, 1979.

Henderson, Lesley, ed. *Twentieth-Century Romance and Historical Writers*. 2nd ed. Chicago: St. James, 1990.

Keating, A.R.F., ed. *Whodunit? A Guide to Crime, Suspense, and Spy Fiction*. New York: Van Nostrand Reinhold Co., 1982.

Knight, Stephen. *Form and Ideology in Crime Fiction*. Bloomington: Indiana University Press, 1980.

Oleksiw, Susan. *A Reader's Guide to the Classic British Mystery*. Boston: G. K. Hall, 1988.

Palmer, Jerry. *Thrillers: Genesis and Structure of a Popular Genre*. New York: St. Martin's Press, 1979.

Index

About the Author

RICHARD C. TURNER is Professor and Chair of the English Department at Indiana University-Purdue University Indianapolis. He has published essays on Milton, Swift, literature and science, and on incorporating historical contexts into the teaching of literature.